WOMEN OF A CERTAIN COURAGE

First published 2025 by
FREMANTLE PRESS

Fremantle Press Inc. trading as Fremantle Press
PO Box 158, North Fremantle, Western Australia, 6159
fremantlepress.com.au

Cover image by Serge Aubert / Adobe Stock
Designed by Carolyn Brown, tendeersigh.com.au
Printed by Everbest Printing Investment Limited, China

A catalogue record for this book is available from the National Library of Australia

ISBN 9781760994457 (paperback)
ISBN 9781760994464 (ebook)

Fremantle Press is supported by the State Government through the Department of Local Government, Sport and Cultural Industries.

Fremantle Press respectfully acknowledges the Whadjuk people of the Noongar nation as the Traditional Owners and Custodians of the land where we work in Walyalup.

WOMEN OF A CERTAIN COURAGE

Edited by Bron Bateman

FREMANTLE PRESS

Trigger warning key

Readers are advised to take care

AB	abuse
ABL	ableism
ABT	abortion
CA	child abuse
DTH	death or dying
DI	deceased Aboriginal or Torres Strait Islander people may be mentioned
DV	domestic violence
HMP	homophobia and heterosexism
MCS	infertility/miscarriages
MT	medical trauma
MLS	mental illness
PRG	pregnancy/childbirth
PSY	psychiatric setting
RCM	racism and racial slurs
SH	self-harm
SA	sexual assault
SXM	sexism and misogyny
SUI	suicide
TRP	transphobia and trans misogyny

Contents

Introduction – Bron Bateman

When Fremantle Press approached me to edit this anthology, I was immediately delighted – both with the opportunity, and particularly the topic. Women and Courage. How much more perfect a subject to explore? I was reminded of Lady Macbeth in Shakespeare's *Macbeth*, saying to her husband before the murder of Duncan: '[b]ut screw your courage to the sticking place and we'll not fail.'

As I began to work on this anthology, I wrote these words on a sticky note on my laptop and prepared for the creative journey of a lifetime.

'Being a woman' and 'courage' are written into our culture as being oppositional – or at least not often remarked upon. The narratives of courage are constructed around the sports ground, the battlefield, or man-versus-mountain survival stories. Courage is often gendered as a masculine experience, grounded in physicality and strength. Yet, even while writing these words I am struck by how audacious and limiting that seems.

When I invited eighteen women to tell me their stories of courage, I hoped for, and received, entirely different narratives.

Women endure the greatest of privations – and these are often embodied, often linked with our roles as parents or parents-to-be, attuned to our reproductive capacity, but also with our capacity to fight for what we believe in; to survive natural disasters; to endure chronic illness, mental and physical. Then there are, of course, the dangers of moving through the world as a woman – compounded by colour, age, sexual orientation, gendered identity – and of being targets of physical violence from men who are strangers, and from men we know.

I knew that the women I asked would have stories of courage, but when I approached them to write an essay, nearly every woman said: 'Oh, but I'm not courageous …'

I told them how they appeared through my eyes, and the eyes of others: the courage they displayed during their experiences as Indigenous women and gender-diverse women, their battles with serious illness, both visible and not openly seen; infertility; domestic violence and sexual abuse; their survival of bushfires and floods; of living with mental illness and institutional and governmental oppression; their survival of violence wrought by partners, or police with guns and horses; their willingness to lay down their bodies in protest.

As the stories of these remarkable women arrived, I found their courage confirmed, and myself moved to tears, by their acts of bravery and survival, their determination to live openly and courageously in a world that preferred they did not exist – and to thrive.

*

Water is a pervasive element in this collection. Trans woman Eliora Avrahami learns to swim from her mother, and survives the currents of abuse as a child, and contends with mental illness as a mother and wife in her adult years, alongside a productive academic career. Sally Scott writes compellingly about near-drowning as a child and caught as an adult in the rips of bipolar disorder and breast cancer. Michelle Sweeney explores the internal impact of the 2022 Lismore floods, trying to hold it together as others who needed her therapy fell apart.

Elder Averil Dean, Reneé Pettitt-Schipp, Cynthia Dearborn and Shannon Meyerkort find their voices and the power of being women in their relationships with the land. Elder Averil survives the steady, excoriating effects of racism experienced by Indigenous people in Western Australia, all the while living a gracious and productive life. Her education of generations of young people is a testament to her endurance as an Aboriginal Elder. Reneé writes movingly of her bond with Aboriginal women and Elders in the 'Save Beeliar Wetlands' protests and their aftermath. After a childhood of silence, Cynthia describes her appearance before the court on charges of criminal trespass and her emerging voice as a lesbian educator in the face of threats of violence. Shannon survives the heartrending danger of Canberra bushfires as a young woman from the city. Her writing bristles with the immediacy of terror and anxiety when life is stripped back to simple survival.

Annamaria Weldon navigates her diagnosis of Parkinson's disease with self-aware determination, explaining how the act of travelling changes her relationship to a degenerative illness. Jo Giles lives with the processes and probability of dying from cystic fibrosis until a double lung transplant offers her a second chance. Through prose and poetry, Esther Ottaway writes about autism in women – the massively underdiagnosed spectrum disorder that is most often viewed through the prism of male experience – and of how she and her daughter have come to flourish in the world.

Anna Jacobson, Penny Jane Burke, Nadia Rhook and Paola Magni explore the personal power and freedom that can be attained through education. Anna is disrupted from a PhD by a controlling psychiatrist until she regains agency through MAD studies and psychiatric survivor activism. Penny Jane escapes the decimating violence of an abusive spouse, driven by her desire to attain higher education and a voice that can liberate both herself and other women. As a historian, Nadia explores the foundations of colonialist Australia and the place where that intersects with her own experiences with infertility and IVF. With scarcely a backward look, Paola Magni leaves her home country, forging her own path as one of the world's foremost forensic scientists.

Natalie Damjanovich-Napoleon is amongst the ten percent of women who experience endometriosis. Its intertwining of pain and doctors' blank refusal to recognise that pain will resonate with many other women. Lisa Collyer's essay confronts domestic violence and what it takes to walk away. She does this through snapshots across time, documenting the impact of many small moments from childhood to adulthood.

The anthology is bookended with the two most confronting and polemic essays of all. These are the pieces by Indigenous lawyer and activist Megan Krakouer, and gender-diverse activist and educator Andrea Thompson.

Megan rails about the hatred and institutional racism inherent in a white, colonialist, patriarchal society, where the removal of Indigenous children from their families continues unabated. She tells us that she speaks not for herself but for all the women she walks beside – the Elders, Aunties, Grandmothers and Mothers – who are left to pick up the pieces of broken lives. Her piece is a clarion call for radical love and radical change.

Andrea describes herself as an ordinary woman but she also happens to be extraordinary – she writes unflinchingly about the deprivations and oppressions of being a trans woman in a predominantly heterosexual society.

The fierceness and resilience of these two women together contain all the other shapes and iterations of courage in between.

The women in this *Women of a Certain Courage* anthology have much to teach us. Their very personal essays speak to the universality of sisterhood. Read their work and know them a little better. Know yourself a little better. As Eliora Avrahami so eloquently writes: 'So here I am, ready to immerse myself. Ready to let go of the past, all of the fear and pain and shame, to find the bravery to accept love as well as give it.'

May all we women carry that kernel of courage in our hearts. To love. To live. To move forward.

The Sisterhood: A Multitude of Voices— Megan Krakouer

AB, CA, DI, DV, RCM, SA, SUI

Megan Krakouer is a Menang Woman of the Noongar Nation, the youngest of thirteen siblings. She is a renowned activist, law reformer, and prominent social justice advocate and arbitrator for the voiceless. Megan is Director of the National Suicide Prevention and Trauma Recovery Project, Director (Wagyl Kaip) of the South West Aboriginal Land and Sea Council and holds a Bachelor of Laws from Deakin University. She works for knowmore, the free, independent legal service, contributing to the Royal Commission into Institutional Responses to Child Sexual Abuse. To ensure voices were heard by the Royal Commission, she visited twenty-seven adult prisons in four states around Australia, as well as more than thirty remote communities. Their stories broke her heart. Megan regularly chairs national suicide prevention conferences and national forums on the issues created by the historical and contemporary sins of this nation. In 2019, Megan travelled to Germany to repatriate to their homelands forty-two ancestors, of which six were brought back to Noongar homeland. Her life's work has at its foundation the desire to use her conviction, heart and dedication to positively help change the narrative for Aboriginal and Torres Strait Islander people.

A multitude of voices

In unconventional manner I live in a binary, the courage of the tens of thousands of girls and women I have met with nowhere to turn. I cannot deny the courage of anyone, by excluding them, of the thousands of boys and men downtrodden who I've met. It is the universal we all seek, equality in all its forms and freedoms.

I do not discuss myself before others, who are yet to acquire privilege. I co-built at first an unfunded service for sisters, brothers, with nowhere to turn but us. We continued through difficult times during the last few years, because we know that so many of our people – particularly sisters and brothers living in poverty – have always felt the ache and harrow of being seen as different. We are the Black Struggle. Where our identity was made a liability, where we were denied being who we are, where we were punished for our very existence, where the sins of those who came to our lands uninvited, without any delay, by force, took our homelands and went about excluding us.

To this day, many of us are still seen as different, and we say this to each other in inherent understanding. Oh, we still understand, we are seen as different. Different Eyes. Therefore, we are The Black Struggle, Different Eyes. So, we have focused our service to those of our people who need us. Where we have resonance, not dissonance. Where we have connection, not disconnection. Where we love, not expect. We do not close 'cases', we do not have a time limit on being there for our sisters and brothers. From the very beginning we have chosen to lead with the memories of sin which wound the affected, the children, the parents, leading with their voices, their stories. We will be there for you.

The majority of the people we support, as it happens, are women, as the intersection of racism and classism is a cesspool, a large subset, where courageous, impoverished women are pitted against judgemental systems in a daily burden to keep close their children, nurture alone their single-parent families and, for many, pick up the pieces for sisters whose children have been removed and take them into their care – a sisterhood of need and sacrifices, for they could have been 'them'. These are women of courage.

Our Black mothers living impoverished or in proximity to poverty are at the forefront of some of the issues which injuriously ache the heart, make identity a liability, scouring demonisations and horrid assumptions of people no-one should endure. This service – the National Suicide Prevention and Trauma Recovery Project – cannot be a nameless sea of words but a light in the dark bringing forth the shadows. Without light, there are no shadows. We together are courage.

This service must also be a dividend of change agency, a lifting of the lid, a spurring of understandings, an opening of the turnpike to reform. We must not nestle into a crafting of sorrow for sorrow's sake. We must not be lassoed, corralled into the tidal waves of silences and in fear of pugnacious, behemoth institutions. Patriarchy was a corral to women, with girls in the holding pens. Many of us, the world over, have broken free but until all of us are free, we must act as if none of us are free. We seek nothing more than equality, and certainly not dominion, or we will be no better than the former patriarchs. We must seek universalisms, raising the bar through equality and to our best selves, not to forms of conquests.

Such described is what we, my First Nations peoples, also seek – universalism, not assimilation and homogeneity; equality and liberation, not disparities and subjugation. We must not hide in endless banalities and torrents of self-centredness, where in cowardly fashion we merely court a seeming endlessness of reports and recommendations. We must not become part of what has been, of what not only fails but which stonewalls and betrays. We let you know: together we can make a difference.

Through austerity and paucity, I know the model of love and courage does not betray nor fail. Let us together spread the love, and walk as much of this earth as we can.

Mothers and stolen children

I cannot begin my propositions of women of courage without mention of my mother – who reared thirteen of us, and I the thirteenth. My mother and father were equals – in all forms desired, ahead of their time. With courage, all my sisters and brothers went forward in understanding we would not live in dominion. We excelled in our liberation. I lead with the courage of the equality my parents lived with one another in generations filled with stark contrasts and consequences.

I am moved by the Black women of courage who, through the muttering depths of crushing poverty, fought departments of child protection which added to their burdens instead of relieving them. These mothers were relentless, many with no-one to turn to, but they succeeded in keeping their families together or in reuniting them. Far too many, mostly single parents, reached out to departments of child protection, presuming them to be family supports. Waves of judgement collectivised within the team that presented itself as family support. But there was no support to families. I emphasise: there was no conscionable support to families. There is a sameness of description by the hundreds of testifiers. I walked alongside. They felt the brunt of obfuscating vicious judgement after reaching out for help from child protection services portrayed as familial supports. But they were in fact confronted by brutally crude psychometrics, algorithms, risk assessments, filtered by discriminatory obscenities such as prejudices, racism, classism.

Far too many of these calls for help descended into cries of despair as parents were trampled by a rapacious culture of blame and fearmongering. Near immediately, children were removed because of perceived risks born of assumptions and prejudices which at no time bore any grim truth.

What I am describing is the Black Struggle to keep our children. I am not arguing for the perfect system, that is never possible. What I am arguing is that we have a century of horrifying rates of malfeasant child removals and yet the rates increase despite the recalcitrant oppressors' apologies. In comparative terms, the oppressor removes children today at rates higher than yesteryear. The oppressors – from government to departmental bureaucrats – act as if imperators.

I have long argued, with child protection, that the balances of proof have no proximal value to judicial equivalents. There is a hideous scaling down to gossipy sinews and the naked eye's narrowmindedness. There has long been crafted an investiture of faith by children's courts in child protection workers – and concomitantly laws have been changed so children's courts reflect the power imbalances with which child protection workers are armoured. There is no like investiture of faith in this dangerous extreme anywhere else. Not even with police and adults before adult courts. If there was a similar investiture in police by adult courts, our already overfilled adult prisons would triple or quadruple their population.

I describe this amoral power imbalance as tyranny. This uncontested investiture of faith in child protection workers effectively silences the voices of mothers, children, families; it further marginalises the affected, the impoverished.

The power imbalance is so huge, it crafts censorship by omission. The power imbalance is acutely traumatising and debilitating.

The removing of children has become a cheap first resort in a climate of fear: take the children away. Poverty has become a crime, as if to argue that an impoverished parent is unfit to rear a child and that an affluent parent is the best fit to rear children. It is our small claim that most First Nations families who live below the poverty line in the lowest quintile of income base, have at some point come to the attention of the child protection authorities. In its rawest terms, think about this: it is a form of modern-day fatalism. The increasing number of families living below the poverty line coming to the attention of child protection is the overarching reason for the climate of fear and the recipe for disaster that has become this manic and frenetic child separation crisis.

Radical Voice(s)

Powerhouse social justice researcher Gerry Georgatos has long estimated that, by 2030, the total number of Black children removed will double. This is catastrophic, but as the doubling we have got to in the present compared to less than a decade ago was also predictively descriptive of catastrophe, so we are living a catastrophe – a humanitarian crisis. The truth is often implausible to the present, and becomes dissociated. When future generations try to unravel the past, when the burden of today is left to the future, those affected today are not just forgotten peoples – it is too late for our present. We did not do enough. We cowered in not being 'radical'. We cowered in not being 'ostracised'. We chose to work futilely from the 'inside' and never go public nor blow the whistle. We chose 'funding' and 'job security' instead of doing everything we could to expose and change systems which are in fact putridly rotten to the core. We are guilty of all the good we did not do and not just the horrible wrongs we did; pretending we have learned from the past or, even worse, pretending we are working towards real change. If we do not act in the present, then of what value are these damnations and indictments of those who are now long gone? Let us speak of truth, and in the journey let us speak of togetherness and love, and then therefore of the redemptive and the restorative. For if we know what is right and we do not do it, and if we know who to help and we do not help them, then who are we and what is this life all about?

As the suffragettes did not compromise on equality, likewise I do not compromise on the perceived radicalism needed for Black mothers to live as equals even in the face of White sisterhood tainted by misunderstood privilege. While there is 'privilege', there are people without. Equality is not genuine. If we knowingly betray those who reach out for help, this is the worst form of cowardice. I chose radicalism like the suffragettes – the liberators.

The reality is that most families that come to the attention of child protection are impoverished and marginalised. Australia's enduring separation crises are escalating. These crises are not born of an evolved village ideology of inalienable birthrights. The escalating crises are not from a protective flow-on effect by non-divisive villagers. The escalating crises are from 'oppressors' foreign to the remnant peoples of villages destroyed by the oppressor. The language of the diabolically outrageous oppressor is not just 'coded' but catastrophically demonising and labelling and divisive. Let the oppressed and their advocates be at liberty to speak back in the language of their suffering and not in reductionist language that compromises truth and allows the oppressor to be unaccountable, reducing the oppressed to beggars.

This is not about fighting fire with fire. It is about truth-telling. It is about contextualisation. It is about Voice(s). It is about keeping families together. The oppressor has institutional firepower. The mostly unrepresented oppressed have only their unheard voices. If voice is all they have then we must amplify their voices.

The ongoing crisis of suicide and incarceration

The oppressor, drunk with power, historically racially profiled – eugenics, segregation, assimilation. Negative flow-on effects from eugenics-geared policies continue, various forms of effective segregation are still realities and assimilation is the only deal – 'swim or sink'. We can 'Blak-enise' assimilation all we want, with proportional Black workforces and 'consultations', but all we do is bring on more assimilation. Resistance is met with our children taken, with jails crammed with our brothers and sisters, with our people jailed at the world's highest rate, suiciding at abominable rates.

It is not just the disproportionality of poverty crushing First Nations families that has led to the record number and rate of children removed and families ruined by dismemberment, but also the targeted imposition of racism as a point of entry that judges Black mothers, fathers and carers. The rate of removal of Black children from their families living below the poverty line on the assumption of perceived risk is many times more than the removal of Brown and White children attributed a perceived risk. The crisis is more than a national problem – it is a stain on the national consciousness and a divisiveness between Black and White, which, despite unveilings of past abominations, despite subsequent apologies, remains inconsolable.

As Gerry Georgatos condemns: one in fifty Australians die by suicide each year. It is a horrific rate. But the abomination of *one in sixteen* First Nations deaths by suicide each year should have long ago galvanised the nation, our governments, to do all they could do – none of which they have done.

As Gerry Georgatos says: one in fifty Australians living have been to prison – that is more than half a million Australians. But when we disaggregate this data, we find that Australia from a racialised lens is the world's mother of all jailers of its First Nations people. Today, *one in six* First Nations Australians alive have been in prison. This is more than 150,00 First Nations people.

The suicide toll, the prison toll, and the child removal toll on our Black children, are indisputably intertwined, fated from the one inkwell. If families were supported when they asked for help, if child protection acted as a familial support, the suicide rate and the incarceration rate of First Nations people would be significantly less. Therefore, the sins of a nation that brought about the need for a Black Struggle and have been the sinful works of one government after another continue in the present.

The ongoing crisis of 'child protection'

My service advocates for the rights of children and families being kept together where possible and, where families have been separated, in fighting for reunification where possible. I cannot leave unreported our major claim that my service has a near 100 percent record in keeping families together where we have supported and advocated for them, or soon after the removal of children we have succeeded in reunification. Our near 100 percent record should serve as a burning condemnation of the fact that no child protection department has a similar record. This speaks to us of systems set up to remove children and a failure per se to support families to remain together. Our claims argue poor methodology, but it is the methodology which has been approved and therefore shows systemic intentionality, the systemics of choice. Modern-day child protection systems and methods remain coded in child removals and not in child supports. In terms of the Black Struggle to keep families together, child protection is seen by the majority of affected First Nations families as a code for assimilation.

Child protection authorities and family services across the nation are increasing the numbers of their personnel each year, churning out more of their service capacity, which is dominated by the removal of children. We are blunt in our claim that these workers may score a quid, but families are the victims. Child protection authorities in our view need families to investigate so they can maintain their large workforce – to investigate, monitor and remove children. Departments must be made accountable and transparent. It is our call that the grimness of suicides in residential care, in out-of-home care, must be published annually and preferably in real time.

These child protection agencies have conjured up monolithic investigation units and never-ending 'care protection services'. The significant layer within these services is Kafkaesque; it is the poor that seem to be the target. The aggregated department of child protection budget across the nation is 9.4 billion dollars. Each year, there is a 'crying poor' by child protection authorities that more funds are needed to monitor vulnerable families. Each year, in every jurisdiction in the nation, child protection budgets increase and subsequently, the number of children removed increases.

When children are removed from their families over alleged emotional abuse and various other reasons, they are seldom provided with adequate healing and restorative therapies. The removal of a child from her or his family is a significant psychosocial hit. It goes straight to the validity of the psychosocial identity; it hurts – and for many this pain is unbearable. For many, the trauma of removal is unresolvable, inescapable, relentless. For some, this trauma is also compounded by multiple composite traumas which may degenerate into disordered thinking and aggressive complex behaviours.

For the most part, child protection and family services should reconsider how they allocate their budgets and focus on genuinely assisting vulnerable families as opposed to the reductionist approach of removing children. Many child protection and family service workers are not skilled in any number of ways that should be requisite, and are ill-qualified and inexperienced. In our interfaces on behalf of families with child protection workers, we have been appalled by the low levels of skills and understanding of workers – by the horrifically and dangerously low level of seasoned expertise.

Most families investigated by child protection authorities can navigate acute socioeconomic pressures – and even various assertive negative behaviours within their homes – including exposure to alcohol abuse, substance abuse and various psychological illnesses. The involvement and over-involvement of underskilled and, in practice, overly judgemental child protection workers does not only fail to assist but compounds vulnerabilities and induces trauma. There is a generated constancy of trauma. People make mistakes, they can wound each other, but empathy and redemptive forgiveness are likely with families, who are in the first instance intensively supported and thereafter left to themselves to work through their lot.

Child protection workers majorly invalidate people, diminish them and most certainly traumatise every family. It is a grim reality that fifteen percent of the Australian population lives below the Henderson Poverty Line, but amongst First Nations Australians, this is at least forty percent with another twenty percent in proximity. Poverty should never be an excuse for the removal of children. It is a grim reality that about ten percent of children live in families affected by substance misuse but still, for most of these families, there is no genuine reason to remove most of the children who are removed. These families are already stressed and instead of being supported through their major stressor – for instance substance misuse to core mental wellbeing – we impose more stressors on family members, and dump painful, sanctimonious and unreasonable expectations on them.

Reduce the child protection budgets, and the child removals will be reduced. Radically reducing the budget will lead to a triage-based approach to at-risk children by the departments. I am obviously stating it appears there is more to be gained by child protection authorities being underfunded rather than overfunded. In general, no society should be over-involved in the lives of families. We argue that reducing child protection budgets is the most obvious immediate solution to radically reduce the shamefully high child removal rates.

The child protection monolith is washing into society stereotypes of parents and children who are being removed as 'drugged-up', as 'drunk', as 'violent' and as 'incompetent.' Most of the parents are none of these. Stereotypes are often misused intentionally. Some children will need foster care, but our experience is that most children removed should have remained with their parents. In the case of the Black Struggle to keep our children, they have been condemned by the reductionist aspiration to remove children to the care of kin. Children removed from their parents are traumatised. Parents who lose their children, even to other kin, are traumatised. The reductionist aspiration that relative or kinship care is the way to go for children is not a solution. Kinship care is the best option for some children for a period, or permanently, but for most children, it is a damaging experience. Sisters and brothers need to be together where possible; this systematic attitude should be so inclined but is not.

Nearly half the children removed are under five years of age, when their form and content is in most need of their biological parents. The removal of a child from her or his family is dangerous. The world is never a perfect place, and institutions should not act out as if it is or should be. The removal of a child can invalidate the individual – and not just disrupt. Prisons are filling at an ever-increasing rate with individuals who, as children, were removed from their parents. It is our view that more than half the prison population were once children removed from their parents, and for the First Nations prison population, about three quarters. It is our view they are the most elevated group vulnerable to suicide and unnatural deaths.

Unless we radically change policies and narratives to authentically work with families instead of tearing them to pieces, the number of children removed and the suicides of these children as adults will increase.

Courage

As First Nations women, we have a relationship to the land. Those that make decisions may have power, but do they have cultural authority? I say: those that hold positions of power but not cultural authority must listen, hear and act with love in their hearts.

The courage we feel comes from our ancestors. As Black women, we stand on the shoulders of great leaders and great warriors. In speaking with truth and conviction, we must never betray those who fought before us. As women, it is incumbent upon us to fight with courage, conviction and love in our hearts. We must be who we are twenty-four seven. We must be a society filled with love, not hatred.

Some refer to me as a rebel, an activist, an agitator. I am a Menang woman who cares about others and who will fight to the end of my days for genuine justice for my people. This is what my ancestors have placed me on this Country to do.

Without courage in your heart, the narrative will never change. You must fight: regardless of the ridicule you may receive, the cruelty you may receive, and the lateral violence – you must stand in your power and listen with purity in your heart. In the famous words of the great Noongar leader Rob Riley: 'You can't be wrong if you are right. You just have to keep fighting.'

Finding Strength—Averil Dean

DI, DV, RCM

I am a proud Cultural Elder with strong spiritual beliefs and connection to the land. I was born in the bush at the Gnowangerup Mission, in Western Australia's Great Southern region, in 1939 and lived there until I was about nine or ten. I discovered my Aboriginality by just being a kid with freedom to embrace the land, which was important to me because that was where my heart was, that was where my feelings were and that was where I discovered a lot about my culture and myself.

Courage is something that starts growing in you when you experience the adversity and racism that your parents faced throughout your early life and see how they handled it with dignity and pride in their cultural identity. Over the span of my life, I have experienced lots of the same challenges. This essay is my reflection on what courage is about.

I had the privilege of being able to experience the strength of our old people who shared a strong connection to the land. Their spiritual strength came from their relationship with nature. It shone through them and gave them the power to overcome adversity and go forward with pride in their cultural beliefs without displaying any bitterness or animosity towards people who had taken over their land. Even as a child, I felt pride in witnessing their dignified silence and love for their people. This is where the pride in my Aboriginality began to make itself known.

Brother Hedley Wright, who formed and ran the mission, fought a lot of red tape and government policies to have families live together, and he won that battle. He helped the Noongars make their own little houses and we lived together as families – we didn't have that separation of being taken away. I come from a really strong family and my parents tried to shield their children from the hardships they were experiencing. My dad was an accepted leader who was always available to help anyone on the mission.

When the Gnowangerup Aboriginal Mission School was first built, it was only a little shelter and the kids had to sit on kerosene tins. They only had school up to Year Three, and if the kids wanted to continue with education, they had to repeat. When I came into the school, the learning was more advanced, but our schooling was pretty flexible. It was a happy place because we were all Noongar kids together and didn't have to worry about whether we could fit in anywhere.

Gnowangerup town was a very racist place, so the mission was a safe haven. When our people went into town to shop, they had to wait outside until white people had finished their shopping. There was no access to the main hospital – we were treated in a lean-to at the back near the morgue. Noongar kids weren't allowed into state schools at that time.

Our people lived by permits. For example, they had to get a permit to go outside the mission to work, and marriage required a permit too. They even needed a permit to 'Take and Kill Kangaroos for Food Purposes Only'[1] – kangaroo was a traditional staple food of our people!

If our people went into town, they had to be out by the six o'clock curfew or the police would come. Police were supposed to be the protectors, but they were the instigators of a lot of violence and oppression towards Noongar people.

Even when family members were hired to do contract work, they were still subject to a great deal of racism. Grandfather and his family, including my dad and brothers, my dad's brothers and their sons, earned their living working long hours, with minimal pay, clearing the land, burning up, grubbing poisonous plants and fencing the farms. But it was Noongar land, for goodness sake!

One story my uncle told was that as a teenager, he had gone to work on a farm in Gnowangerup as a shedhand with two white men. He was subject to the embarrassment of having his lunch put in the chook pen for him to eat, while the white men were taken into the house. He left the food and walked home. However, some landowners acknowledged their contribution and treated them, as a working family, with respect.

Hearing these stories and seeing how Elder family members kept their dignity and pride in their Aboriginality had a real impact on me, and I have carried it with me my whole life. They have made me a stronger and more resilient person and a proud Aboriginal woman. Witnessing how they survived and kept their spiritual strength when materially they had almost nothing, showed me the true meaning of courage.

My paternal grandfather, Eddie Womber (Williams), always said he was a proud Menang person from Albany. He married my grandmother Lilly, a Burchill from the Salt River area. She was a carrier of wisdom, who became a much-loved Elder in Gnowangerup. Granny gave so much love to all her grandchildren, including me – this became part of my growth as a giver of knowledge.

When the mission started to close down and public schools became accessible to Noongar kids, our family moved a little further west to the Tambellup area, working on farms and camping in the bush. We went to school in Tambellup, catching a school bus. It was very different attending a white school as an Aboriginal child. You always felt you were being judged by what you wore and how you acted. At the school, we suffered racial slurs like 'nigger' and 'boong'. Even small children used these terms.

At the school one day, I met two little kids and the boy said, 'Oh, look, there's a nigger now.' And I went up and slapped him. That was our only defence. No-one wanted to listen to us. No-one cared about what happened. The boy didn't say it again.

But I made some great friends at Tambellup Primary School – they are still my friends, my wonderful friends. You tend to rise above the racist comments when you meet people who have good hearts, and you look for those sorts of people in your life. At Tambellup school we started to get our learning together with the help of some teachers. I had a teacher who looked after me, so I was okay.

My youngest brother badly injured his ankle in a bicycle accident and needed to be urgently taken to Katanning Hospital for treatment. My dad went to one of the farmers that our family had done a lot of work for to ask if he could take him to the hospital. The farmer said yes, but when he came to pick us up, he had spread dirty old grain bags over the back seat for us to sit on. I saw the expression on my dad's face and was so impressed by his dignified silence because of the need to have his young son get urgent treatment.

My dad said to us as children that this was no longer our land because these people had taken it over. He said that the only way that you could be successful and compete with them at their level was through education. For somebody who'd never had formal education, he was a very learned man. And he had this insight into what was the important thing for us in our lives – education. So we were never allowed to miss school.

I pay tribute to my mum, Elsie Williams (née Hayward). She was a great lady. As kids, I guess we all tend to take our mums for granted and don't think about the impact they have on our lives. Mum taught me the importance of being patient and non-judgemental and looking for the good in people. She went through times of domestic violence but still saw the value of being in a stable relationship for the benefit of her children. With the hardship of living in a difficult era, her courage shone through.

My mum worked incredibly hard, helping to clear the land and do the tasks that men did, and yet she still mothered us eleven kids. She would sit all day on a dam bank, washing clothes and boiling them in a kerosene bucket to keep the whites white. It wasn't till I got a bit older that I realised, with admiration, the sacrifices she made for us to enrich our lives.

*

The Department of Native Affairs made regular checks on Aboriginal kids' progress at school and singled out kids they felt would benefit from going away to school in Perth. The idea was to breed out the Aboriginality and teach them to live like white people and get rid of the bush culture that was part of their lives.

The welfare officer focused on me and my brother in Tambellup school and asked my dad if we could go to school in Perth. He was adamant that he wasn't going to send his kids anywhere. They persevered and in the end my dad relented, and said, 'Alright, I'll let her go if you take her sister with her.' So that's how my sister Treasy and I went to Perth.

We stayed in Alvan House, a hostel in Mount Lawley, and went to Girdlestone High School. We wore a collar and tie and a beret and pleated skirt. Being dressed in full school uniform was, at first, a cultural shock. I think they hoped we would forget our Aboriginal culture.

One day my dad came up to the school – he came to the back gate to attract our attention at lunchbreak. Treasy and I went down to him, and he was dressed up in his old suit pants and coat, and they were all clean. He was this Noongar and we were dressed up like white kids, you know. And I felt such a rush of love for this person. He was the most important person in my life – I felt such a rush of love. And I think that's where my pride in who I was and who I will always be came to the fore. I was just so proud to be part of his life. He was a leader and his work ethic achieved better conditions for his own people and especially for his children. I saw that he was afraid of nothing. He was the most courageous person I knew. He also had a wonderful softness. When he came home from the bush he would bring a little bunch of wildflowers for the first child who greeted him.

In the hostel, all the Aboriginal girls were taught how to adjust to life in white society – they made us polish floors and do other domestic chores. If the work was not done to their satisfaction, we had to redo it. Near the end of our school life, they put us in a factory to work while we waited to go into nursing aide training at Royal Perth Hospital.

During our training at Royal Perth, I felt that we did not gain enough hands-on experience and so lacked confidence in our own ability to deliver more in-depth nursing care.

After our training, they offered the trainees a position at Broome Hospital because it was short-staffed. So my friend Verna and I took the plunge and said we would go. Two young Noongar girls on their first plane ride, not knowing anything about the local cultural protocol or the language, or how the people would react to us – it was scary.

*

After our arrival, on the first night, I had to go on duty by myself at the hospital. That scared the life out of me because I didn't know enough then. Coping with the diversity of things that happen in a country hospital was very character-building. When the flu epidemic came into Broome, the hospital was filled with Traditional people from remote communities. I was scared at the time because I didn't know their cultural protocol, but I witnessed the same cultural pride that makes us one people.

Verna was more outgoing and soon made friends with Aboriginal staff who worked in the hospital. So we got to meet the wonderful Aboriginal people in Broome who welcomed us into their community as family. I met my husband, Kenneth Dean, and he became an important part of my life. We married and had two children before moving back to my Country, where he became part of a powerful working team.

In the late 60s, Kenny got a job in Cranbrook, about an hour's drive north of Albany, so we moved our family and that became our home for twelve years. Because of Kenny's strong work ethic, he earned deep respect from the people of Cranbrook. It was like going to a different place because they accepted us and our children as part of the community. So life there was good. When my children began going to school, I encouraged them to always feel pride in who they were and to hold their heads high. I wanted to be their biggest support, and to make the pathway easier for them to tread.

Soon after settling back on Country, I joined with three other strong women, my sister Treasy being one, to attend statewide meetings to fight for better housing, education and living conditions for our people. Over time we have seen some success for our dreams and I'm proud to say I was part of the strength of those women who blazed the way for our people in general.

The opportunity of a housing loan saw us move to Albany because we felt it would be beneficial to our children. We settled in Mount Lockyer and put our children into Mount Lockyer Primary School. Soon after, my brother Jack and his wife, Joan, also moved to Albany. Jack became a much sought-after cultural teacher. If it wasn't for Jack's knowledge and mentoring, I would not have had the courage to become a cultural high school speaker myself. Jack always made me feel that as we shared the same history, I had as much to give as he did. This contributed to my personal growth.

There was a teacher at Albany Senior High School who was putting out feelers for Noongar speakers to do cultural studies with the Year Nines. So Jack and I started there in about 1992. We were joined shortly afterward by our sister Treasy. We used to go once a week. We took all the students on excursions to sites around the districts of Gnowangerup and Tambellup, and Jack would talk about the significance of the sites and what they meant to us as Noongar people. I still work with the schools as a cultural teacher.

When we started cultural studies in the high school, Aboriginal students were embarrassed and tried to distance themselves from our teaching and hoped they wouldn't be seen, but as it continued, we witnessed big changes and saw cultural pride growing in those same students. Whenever we came into the school grounds, they would greet us with love and respect.

Many years after working in the high school, I went to Perth and I was in the Westpac bank in St Georges Terrace, waiting to be served, when I was tapped on the shoulder. I looked around and there was this young white man. He had a suit on and a pink tie that stood out. He was a handsome young man. And he said to me, 'Oh, you're Averil?' And I said, 'Yes.' And he said, 'You won't know me, but I was in your class at Albany Senior High

School and did your cultural learning. You know what,' he said, 'out of my whole school learning journey, yours was the best.' That was my reward.

I held strong views on law-breaking and the need for punishment, but as a community leader, I was persuaded to become an Aboriginal visitor at Albany Regional Prison. My first reaction was, 'Is this me? I shouldn't be here.' However, when I got to know the inmates and began building trust, I warmed towards them, and it became a place that I looked forward to visiting. I was addressed as Aunty, Nan and, to some, even Mum. I felt the inmates' warmth and respect and could show them love and care when anyone was grieving or having problems. I could give them advice and a feeling of self-worth. After fourteen years of employment, my own growth and self-esteem reached great heights and I look back with much satisfaction and pride at my time there.

As a Menang and Goreng Elder, I have a strong cultural connection to the land – it is part of my spirit, part of me. I have a strong connection to my Dreaming and my cultural obligations. I am an accepted speaker and mentor for my people in the Great Southern area. I don't need to prepare a written speech – I believe that spiritual guidance gives me a voice. I speak truthfully about what has happened in my life and share stories that I have been told by my Elders. People tell me that my speeches are inspirational.

I am not afraid to voice an opinion. Courage comes from the heart, and I feel that I connect with people through my speaking – it's one of my strengths. I can be the leader that I want to be because my love of communicating has gained me acceptance. I feel that my courage is valued, but most of all I want people to feel my happiness and love of life.

How Women Shaped the World at the Beeliar Wetlands—Reneé Pettitt-Schipp

DI, RCM

Everything reduces to this: the sensation of muscle pushing against muscle, the fusion of sweat and intimacy of scent, as the police horse pushes against my chest. The horse and I are forced so tightly against one another in the crush of the crowd, I can only see a blurred close-up of her mottled coat. The press of her power against my body makes me fall silent.

The crowd and I step back. In the fine hairs of my cheek, I can now feel the horse's breath. The rhythm of her lungs exudes a warm balm steeped with a scent of damp grasses. I lift my head, and though her snout is forced against my face, she looks down, holds my gaze. Together we breathe while all around us people shout and heave.

'Move back!' the officer yells from high on his saddle, and the horse's head turns, her neck a mobile pillar that causes those of us beneath to duck and weave. The crowd has linked arms so we cannot be singled out by the officers, yet this unified move means we are unable to slip through the gaps in the line of police and horses. Though we can see the trees we so desperately need to protect, they are cordoned off from us by recently erected steel fencing, beside which sits the stark form of a bright-yellow bulldozer. Locked in this stand-off, people begin calling and singing, police poker-faced or yelling.

Finally, the call is made to leave and we let go of each other's arms. The crowd of protesters turns around and walks back along the suburban street, away from the bushland, the trees, the yellow bulldozer. A woman shouts something from behind a flywire door. A man with a TV camera turns his lens my way and I find I cannot hold my mouth straight; my lips begin to quiver, my eyes water. I can still feel the horse's breath warm on my cheek. I turn away from the camera.

As we walk up the hill, the police on horseback get ahead of us, and as they pass, I notice the horses' broad hooves, their shining coats. The mounted officers round the corner, then position themselves at the top of a steep embankment alongside the main road. At the western end of the cordoned-off bushland, the police on foot form a new line, all in high-vis vests, tasers ready at the hip. As we walk to join the other protesters further down the slope of the road's embankment that overlooks the bushland, the group begins to cheer. The officers in the line tense, move back and forward, back and forward, bodies straining, arms raised to their waists.

Some people begin to move down the embankment toward the fence-line, beyond the wall of officers, to where other protesters sit and rest in the shade of a singular tree or stand chatting in groups. The police on the shining horses see them and begin to move quickly across sunlit grass in their direction. Those sitting see the mounted officers rapidly approaching and begin to scramble to their feet. The officers do not stop, instead they ride their steeds into the group while turning the horses' bodies, using the creatures' bulk to push men and women to the ground. One officer looks down at a young man who has fallen, spurs his horse forward, and I bring my camera to my eye just as he forces the horse's hooves over the man's sprawled body. People begin to panic and cry out, moving quickly back up the bank. Others bend down to help the man who now seems frozen, face bleeding from a cut just above his eye. At the top of the bank, rally coordinators call for calm into red plastic megaphones. Someone with a guitar starts to sing.

*

Even now as I type these recollections of the protests that escalated between December 2016 and March 2017 at the Beeliar Wetlands in Perth's southern suburbs, the trauma of the events that unfolded over four months in my local community sits like a bruise beneath my skin. At the end of this day of intense confrontation near Walliabup (Bibra Lake), unable to completely walk away from the brutality of what was unfolding, I stood at a distance on the road's embankment. From here I could see the media interviewing the man with the bleeding head as protesters who had made it inside the wire were arrested, some dragged away then loaded into the backs of police wagons. A car was escorted into the fenced area as the police formed a line in front of the bulldozer. A man walked from the car to the bulldozer. The sergeant gave the instruction, and the man started the machine's engine. The driver steered the bulldozer toward a large, branching she-oak, carefully lowering the machine's blade toward the tree's base. The bulldozer groaned as it strained to sever the tree from the earth, the she-oak's limbs began to quiver and spasm. The sky cracked with a ripping sound as the tree was wrenched from its roots, its broad body falling behind the metal shape of the machine.

*

These scenes were part of the Roe 8 protests – an organised resistance to the Barnett State Government plan to extend Roe Highway through bushland in the Beeliar Wetlands, not far from the port town of Fremantle in Western Australia. The Beeliar Wetlands are the most significant site of Aboriginal heritage in Perth south of the Swan River. It is an important site of the Waugal, Firestick and Spirit Children Dreaming.[1] As the late Aboriginal Elder and activist, Judy Jackson shares:

> It's a sacred site Bibra Lake and North Lake. It was an area where a lot of the historic stories of the invasion came from … the destruction of the camps … the murder of the Aboriginal people in the area … [It was also] where the main corroborees concerning the area were carried out … it is a very important place.[2]

Directly in line with the proposed freeway's path, where ancient banksias cast enormous, jagged shadows and arching paperbarks ghost the greenery, sits a sacred Noongar birthing site.

In addition to the state's Indigenous heritage, the Beeliar Wetlands are an integral part of the small number of Perth's wetlands that have survived on the Swan Coastal Plain; over eighty percent of Perth's wetlands have been destroyed since colonisation.[3] The Beeliar Wetlands contain nine distinct ecological communities (some endangered), and over 198 fauna species, 177 species of native birds and are home to nine rare and endangered species including peregrine falcon, graceful sun moth, southern brown bandicoot, king spider orchid, and the red-tailed and white-tailed black cockatoo.[4] The fight for the Beeliar Wetlands has been taking place for more than thirty years.

*

In *Being and Nothingness*, Jean-Paul Sartre tells us that when we act, we alter the shape of the world.[5] When we take an active role in response to events in our communities, our acts can be overt and direct: speaking out, protesting, writing letters to the paper, blockades and door-knocking. However, sometimes our actions can be almost imperceptible: bearing witness, humour, fostering connection, growth in our capacity to love, slow expansions of self. It can also be the sustenance of, and commitment to, stories we know to be true. Though subtle, these acts also fundamentally alter the shape of our world. At the Beeliar Wetlands, we did both kinds of 'acting', and I believe this is what made our campaign so extraordinarily successful, the subtler actions often driven by the courage and creativity of women in our community.

The campaign to save the Beeliar Wetlands began to galvanise when convenor Kate Kelly stood up and actively took on a leadership role, a role that came at enormous physical and emotional cost, but that ultimately brought together a disparate group of people from all walks of life. We were driven in in our conviction that Roe 8 was not in the community's best interest. We also knew that Fremantle port (the route's ultimate destination) only had a lifespan of around ten years before it reached capacity and another port would need to be built; it made no economic sense to spend two billion dollars[6] to serve a port with such a finite future.

Under Kate's leadership, protesters became strategic. Non-violent direct-action training was organised and a roster drafted so the protest site could be monitored every day from dawn until dusk. As the protesters' presence and resolve increased, so did the numbers of police, often disproportionately. Lawyers and journalists volunteered their time as the matter was dragged through the courts. Victories were won, then overturned, but the legal process bought the protest movement time and, most importantly, exposure, drawing more and more people toward the campaign to save some of Perth's last remaining wetlands.

On 8 November 2016, the shock announcement of US President Donald Trump's victory was broadcast across the world's screens. I believe this was a turning point for the Roe 8 campaign. People everywhere saw the cost of complacency, and many of us were very worried for our world. The numbers of protesters surged as people who would not normally be involved in protests understood what was at stake. I distinctly remember seeing one protester at this time with a sign that read 'Things are so bad, even the introverts are here!'

On 5 December, the Save Beeliar Wetlands group lost its last avenue of appeal against the project in court. A shift began to take place in the police force, the officers becoming increasingly violent and confrontational; that same day, move-on notices were given to sixty people gathered at the protest. On 11 December the police started making arrests, and sudden and rapid clearing of the area began. The clearing was so swift that the government was ignoring its own protocols,[7] meaning vulnerable and threatened species such as the southern brown bandicoot were recorded as being crushed to death in the process.

By 20 December, four hundred protesters had gathered at the site daily. On 5 January 2017, at 5.30 in the morning, more than a thousand people gathered at the construction site. People became united and emboldened, witnessing the sheer scale of resistance to the project. Sensing the shift, a handful of protesters seized the moment and pushed over the fence that separated the bushland from the crowd. Tentatively at first, and then in huge numbers, people crossed the fence-line and surrounded the bulldozer compound. The police panicked, began singling out and arresting the protesters and (as in the scene already depicted) forced their horses into the crowd. The protest went all day, police resources were absolutely stretched, yet by sunset, swathes of rare and precious bushland had been decimated before our eyes.

*

In their compelling work *Active Hope*, renowned deep ecologist Joanna Macy and author Chris Johnstone tell us that it is a revolutionary act to bow to our grief and what we are losing, yet when we do, we experience connection, belonging and delight.[8] Many of us at the Beeliar protest came in and out of coping; there were days when many of us struggled to hold onto hope. However, as we watched each other's creative and courageous acts, we became more creative and courageous ourselves. The more aggressive the police became, the more expansive the community's responses, and the more deeply we experienced our connections to one another. Psychologist Mary Pipher describes the process of moving beyond environmental grief and back into affirmative action as 'transcendent coping'.[9]

The courageous and creative acts of protesters were many and varied, from children forming love-heart sculptures from small stones at the feet of police to an artist painting a mural on a wall in a public park of premier Colin Barnett driving a bulldozer into Carnaby habitat. Wetland poetry readings took place in the path of earth-moving machinery and a protester dressed as a white-tailed black cockatoo repeatedly interrupted Barnett's media interviews on the campaign trail for the forthcoming state election. One of the most successful and playful initiatives occurred at the renowned Swim Thru Rottnest opening at Cottesloe Beach (the premier's electorate and heartland). Colin Barnett was opening the event and all major media outlets were covering the gathering. Cleverly disguising themselves as swimmers on the day, a group of female protesters penned *drowning in debt* and *put Libs last* down their arms (made to look the same as the Rottnest swimmers' registration numbers) then arranged for media to take their photo with Barnett. The image of a beaming, oblivious premier flanked by attractive and subversive young women in their bathers, went viral.

However, one of the most striking examples of connectivity and transcendent coping during the campaign was the leadership exhibited by Indigenous women. Indigenous people were at the forefront of the fight to save the Beeliar Wetlands, despite the incredible personal risk involved (there have been more than 550 Indigenous deaths in custody since the Royal Commission into Aboriginal Deaths in Custody in that concluded in 1991[10]). Indigenous women held healing ceremonies for those who struggled to cope with trauma of what was unfolding, and at the height of acts of police and state violence, an extraordinary and deeply moving event took place.

*

It is a Sunday morning in the middle of summer. The wetlands are drying and the wildflowers have finished their seasonal flush of colour; trees scatter spent leaves. Through the forest and around the edge of Coolbellup (also known as North Lake), just beyond the protest site, women are walking. In complete silence, well over a hundred women walk, Indigenous and non-Indigenous, shoulder to shoulder, the rhythm of their footfall a soft drumbeat on the earth. The women's silence settles over lake beds and reeds, paperbarks and eucalypts. White-tailed black cockatoos call, hidden in distant canopy. Beyond the lake, the line of women continues, snakes through the sand; around them a warm wind stirs. At Frog Swamp the line stops, and the women wait on the dry lake bed, forming a circle, standing arm in arm. More women arrive and the silence is gently broken as the circle widens in an effort to contain the sheer number of bodies gathered in the space.

'Thank you for coming,' one of the women begins. 'We want you to know we can see your pain and we thank you for being here with us today, working with us to protect this sacred land. But while your hearts are breaking over this particular site, you need to understand that this is what happens to Aboriginal people all the time. We are sorry for your loss, but losing our sacred sites is what happens to us all of our lives. Please try and understand the suffering our people endure; it is a grief that does not end. It is so important to understand this as we come together united today.'

A woman with a guitar comes forward and begins to teach us a song, 'Dabakarn Nidja Bilya' – go slowly here, river/umbilical cord.[11] Slowly the song swells as the crowd of women begins to sing, over a hundred women raising their voices in Noongar, the language of the land. In this moment of song, in the absence of police and away from machines, something in us – for a moment – is made whole.

*

The impact of the solidarity I experienced with Indigenous women during the protests led directly to my decision to lock myself to a banksia near the birthing site on the highway's proposed route; I could not stand by as a male politician (with full knowledge of the area's significance) ordered bulldozers to destroy a women's sacred site. Many women, including myself, were arrested and briefly imprisoned at this time, the highway's destruction successfully delayed for two days.

The morning the bulldozers finally rolled into the birthing site, I could not attend the protest due to my bail conditions, and I was grateful. I watched on social media as women sang a lament in the rain as bulldozers pushed over two- or three-hundred-year-old trees, causing some of the police officers in the line-up to cry. The late Noongar Elder Reverend Sealin Garlett shared the significance of this area in this way:

> Many years ago this piece of land was set aside as a birthing place ... The [women] could stay there for a number of days, even weeks, and be provided for ... They never took more than was needed, and it was always there to provide their needs and to look after them [and] they cared for the land ... this place here goes deeper than just being a place of birth. Just being a place of origin. This place ... brings the deep identity that we Aboriginal people have with this land.[12]

Today, due to the protests, much of the birthing site has survived. Among the devastation, sacredness remains. The Barnett government completely underestimated the power of the people to write their own futures, even if we had to do it daily and with our own bodies, and even when it came at an incredible personal price for those involved. During that time, we were neglectful parents, worn-out workers and exhausted partners. However, finally, at the March 2017 state election, almost exactly two months after a thousand people pushed through a steel barrier that sought to separate a community from Country, the Barnett government was voted out. The destruction of the wetland for the highway came to an end.

Shortly after the election, Noongar women invited those women who were arrested at Beeliar to be involved in a ceremony down at South Beach. On the beach, a stand of trees from the wetlands knocked over during the construction for the proposed highway was placed upright and lit up as we walked together around the flames. In front of a large crowd, we lifted our voices, singing 'Dabakarn' once again. But as the sky filled with a gentle haze of rain, the trees would not burn. The setting sun filled the sky around us with an orange brilliance. A rainbow formed over the head of Elder George Walley as he stepped onto a sand dune to speak to the crowd, and he told us this was the crying rain, the healing rain. It was over now, and the unseasonal shower had come to cleanse us of everything that had happened so we could heal and start over again.

So much was lost at the Beeliar Wetlands: pristine habitat for threatened and endangered species such as the white-tailed back cockatoo and the oblong turtle, as well as the partial destruction and violation of ancient and sacred sites so important to Noongar people. Yet what we gained was hope and an experience of our power, a courageous story in which Aboriginal and non-Aboriginal Australians came together: grandmothers and children, lawyers and musicians, academics and retirees. We became the creators, players and orators in the narratives told about our home and our communities; together we sustained stories about what was sacred in our lives.

Under Fire—Shannon Meyerkort

We move to Canberra at the tail end of 2002. Though Perth born and bred, as newlyweds, we have been living in Sydney since early 2000. When we pack our car and drive the three hundred kilometres from the lush green coastal suburbs of Sydney, it is to a parched capital city in the grip of severe drought.

We drive in almost complete silence, weighed down by the enormity of what we are doing. We are leaving behind our carefree life of renting an ancient red-brick apartment for a heavily mortgaged townhouse in the southern Canberra suburbs. We are leaving behind friends and colleagues from the university where we worked, Sydneysiders who taught us how to drink VB without irony and the joy of sour cream and sweet chilli on a bowl of wedges. We are leaving behind our adopted city where the sun rises over water and sets over land, where the electricity of the Olympics still lingers.

I hadn't been afraid to make the move from Perth to Sydney: it felt like an extended holiday, an adventure. It feels different moving to Canberra, like the party is over and we're now expected to start acting like grown-ups. Our single-level townhouse is part of a large complex at the foot of the hills, a neighbourhood of curling cul-de-sacs like legs on a spider. The grass crackles underfoot and the garden needs a decent watering, but we feel like adults as we walk through the front door of our first home.

Even the barrage of bills that follows cannot dent my enthusiasm for this new stage of life.

In early January we welcome family from Perth. West Australians are no strangers to long, hot summers, but there we have the deep blue ocean on our doorstep and the Fremantle Doctor sea breeze to bring relief. Landlocked, the Canberra air suffocates. Still new to the city, we play host to our tourists, exploring as they do, seeing our new home through their eyes.

Late one afternoon, I take our guests trekking into the nearby Urambi Hills Nature Reserve, gently ridged hills straight out of an English storybook, except with the colours all wrong. It is a place to make you feel small yet connected. Like an ocean in turmoil, the hills become bigger, rolling into the Brindabellas, cresting in the distance with Mount Tennent.

Canberra is called the Bush Capital for a reason. The city and suburbs are dwarfed by the enormous national parks that curl around its western and southern flanks, and the bush winds its long fingers between the cracks, with verdant green stretching through the suburbs right into the heart of the city. Standing with friends at the top of the hill that afternoon, we have no inkling what will be coming over the ridge in the days ahead. It is silent, except for the crunch of dried grass beneath our feet, the sky bleached of colour, a pent-up stillness in the hills as if the world is just waiting.

*

On Wednesday 8 January, just over the border in New South Wales, lightning strikes ignite four small fires. If it's reported in the news, no-one pays much attention.

*

Australia is scorched by fifty thousand bushfires every year. The most destructive are given names, usually based on the day they occurred: Black Friday, Ash Wednesday, Black Sunday. Since 1851, more than eight hundred people have been killed by bushfires, but this relatively small number obscures the extent of the devastation.

The lingering effects of a bushfire can last years, burned into the memories of entire communities. I'm terrified of house fires thanks to a traumatic event in my early childhood, but I'm not afraid of bushfires because, in my mind, bushfires don't happen in cities.

*

We wave goodbye to our guests, letting them escape back west to a summer of a different colour, of blues and yellows and blinding white. The approaching bushfires have also escaped. The four small fires have merged and are now burning just beyond the horizon. But the sky is still clear and we haven't heard the whispers of what will come.

When the kangaroos arrive in search of a meal, I watch them through the kitchen window as they forage in the scrappy grass that runs through the centre of our complex. It may be slim pickings but the grass is still better than that of their habitat in the hills. As a city kid, it scares me a little to see the enormous animals make their way between the rubbish bins and children's bikes. Later we realise that we should have seen it as a warning.

*

On Saturday 18 January, the forecast is for hot, windy, and dry conditions, and I plan to hide from it. My husband is studying, and I want to spend the day in the dark, watching *Gone With the Wind* in its entirety. I pull down the blockout blinds in the lounge and settle in. Midmorning, right when Atlanta is burning, a knock comes at the door. Katrina, my neighbour, stands there. We share a driveway. She lives with her ten-year-old daughter,

Emily, and a menagerie of rabbits and dogs. Usually she seems amused by our city ways, but today she is worried for us.

'What's your plan?' she wants to know.

I hit pause. 'My plan for what?'

She pushes the screen door back and gestures at me to follow her. Outside I am met with an alien landscape – the sky has clouded over and is tinged with a dusty red. The smoke is thick in my throat. It might be the smoke or it might be panic, but my chest is tight and I turn to her, needing her maternal calm. Over my shoulder, I can see the twin rounded mounds of the hills. They are only a few streets away, the grassy slopes butting right up to the fences of houses, the bush continuing unchecked for hundreds of kilometres. A bush that is on fire.

I am not prepared. I have no clue.

If Katrina is afraid, she doesn't let it show. But her courage is not the absence of fear, it is action in the face of it. She gives us a plan – a quick trip to the shop to purchase supplies: tennis balls to block the gutters, a hose to flood them, bottled water, a battery-operated torch.

My husband and I pile into the car with our neighbours. I sit in the back with Emily, jittery with excitement and relief that we are doing something. Many others have had a similar idea, with crowds three deep in the garden section, hands reaching for tubes of balls. Warnings come over the loudspeaker of the shopping centre, startling us with their loudness.

'It's for the people in the movie theatres,' Katrina says. 'They will have no idea what's happening.'

When we emerge from the chill of the shopping centre, the sky has a hellish red glow. The heat sucks the breath from my body, while strong winds whip at our hair and clothes.

At home, we change into our least flammable shirts and pants, flood the gutters, fill the sinks. We pack a suitcase of our most precious things. On top of clothes and books, I lay a quilt I have been sewing. My husband packs his textbooks. Katrina tells us to take the car out of the garage and reverse it into the drive ready for a speedy escape, as she has done. We do as we are told, not considering that if we both try to leave at the same time in a panic, our cars will collide in our shared drive.

*

When a fire burns hot enough, it releases vast quantities of smoke, ash and heat, significant enough to change the atmosphere above it. In effect, the fire creates its own weather pattern: enormous pyrocumulonimbus clouds, or supercell thunderstorms. These can have winds up to 250 kilometres per hour and generate their own lightning. Erratic winds beneath the storm cloud bring bursts of swirling dry air down to the fire, whipping up embers and carrying them vast distances in all directions, starting a new family of fires.

What roars into Canberra at 4 p.m. on Saturday 18 January is no longer a bushfire or even a pyrocumulonimbus. Releasing more energy than the bomb that flattened Hiroshima, it leaves a trail of devastation half a kilometre wide and twenty-five kilometres long. It blows roofs off houses, uproots enormous trees, flips over trucks, and flattens plantations, incinerating everything in its wake.

A name will later be given to such an event: a fire tornado.

*

By unspoken agreement, my husband and I know we want to stay in the company of our motherly neighbour. Her no-nonsense approach takes the edge off my nerves. We play cards in the front room of her house with one eye on the television, which is never turned off. There is little news available, although we can hear helicopters flying overhead. It is stifling inside her townhouse; rickety fans push smoky air around the room while we rub ice cubes on our arms. We are waiting, but we don't know what we are waiting for. After a while, Katrina grows restless and suggests she and my husband go to buy some cold beer. It feels like a very Australian response to a crisis, liquid courage. I nod in agreement, yet inside my head I am screaming for them not to leave.

With our protectors gone, Emily and I mute the television and the two of us sit in the front window, waiting for their return. We do not speak or move a muscle until we hear a tinkling sound on the roof.

Emily turns to me with hopeful eyes. 'Rain?' she asks.

It sounds like rain to me as well. Clasping hands, we run out the back. Beneath the tin roof of the verandah, the sound is so loud we cannot hear ourselves speak. But the smell is wrong. We step out the back gate into the scrappy laneway and tilt our faces to the sky. What falls into my outstretched hand makes my stomach clench. Burned leaves, blacker than night, fall from the sky as if we are in a Tim Burton movie. Even if only one of these falling leaves is still burning, I know it can bring the bushfire right into our backyard.

When my husband and neighbour return twenty minutes later, she with a carton of beer in her arms, I think I see the flames in their eyes. Trees are alight on both sides of the road, my husband says. Our street is an enormous cul-de-sac with only one way in and one way out, and the bush surrounding the entrance is already burning. Katrina says if we want to evacuate, we need to go now. But we are a few streets back from the bush and have nowhere else to go. So we stay.

I pick up the portable phone to call my mother in Perth. It is late afternoon but inside and out, it is dark as night, backlit by a terrifying red glow.

She answers on the first ring.

I tell her calmly about our plan to stay, although the car is already packed. She tells me she has been watching the television, that houses in Kambah have already been lost. I try to reassure her – I don't want her worrying about being three thousand kilometres away and powerless to help. I try to make her laugh with the stories of the beer and the falling leaves. It's not funny.

'Mum,' I say eventually, trying to hold back tears. 'I'm scared.' The moment the words leave my mouth, the line goes dead. The lights go out. The first of many fires has begun ripping through powerlines and infrastructure in the heart of our capital. I try calling back, but there is no dial tone, only silence.

There is nothing I can do to appease my mother's worry now. We are disconnected, an island in a sea of flames. I stand on the front drive watching in terror. To the west, the Urambi Hills are on fire. The drought has left an absence of underbrush, and hungry rabbits and kangaroos left a dearth of long grass. The hills glow as though covered in thousands of fireflies, spots of fire with a roar of orange in the distance behind. To the east, the fire has crossed the Tuggeranong Parkway and is crawling up the sides of Mount Taylor. Behind us, to the north, Mount Arawang explodes in a ball of flames.

When the fire rushes into Canberra, it no longer has a single front. It has broken into a thousand smaller fires, jumping ahead in ember attacks like children playing leapfrog. After more than a week of burning slowly, being watched and monitored by the fire services of two states and territories, it catches everyone off guard as it flies over the last twenty kilometres in less than an hour.

*

The large corner block we share with our neighbour makes us central to two streets, and people begin amassing at the end of our drive, a ragtag community of young and old, families and singles. Our slightly elevated block has an absence of tall trees and buildings, and we can sit watching all directions. We are mostly strangers, but we now share a common experience. There has been no power for hours, and in the eerie red darkness we sit on lawn chairs and upturned crates, sharing food that would otherwise go to waste. As we sip lukewarm beer, there is mostly silence, just the sombre voice of a local radio announcer providing updates on the fire. Every noise, every crackle makes me jump. I am ready to run, but I have nowhere to hide.

A cool change comes around 7 p.m. and the radio tells us the worst has passed. Everything that can burn has already been burned. My body aches and spasms as I try to relax from a state of prolonged tension. The ominous glow over the rooftops has faded, the spots of fire on the hills dull and die, but we stay wary and alert. Eventually our watches tell us it is time for bed. We cannot see the moon or stars through the thick layer of smoke that blankets us, but we cautiously retreat to our darkened houses. By torchlight, we try washing the pungent smell from our skin.

When I blow my nose, the tissue is stained black, and I am suddenly back in my grandparents' Padbury home after a house fire. A memory I have been repressing all day comes back and the relief I feel is ferocious and visceral as I collapse onto the ground and finally cry. My husband and I crawl into bed, tangle ourselves into each other, knowing that sleep will be impossible.

*

The world we wake to the following day is quieter, more solemn. The birds do not sing, and there is little traffic humming on the parkway. I feel exposed and raw. The violent red sky has receded, leaving behind a smoky grey haze that lingers on my hair for days and in my memory for years. I tread gently, as though the ground itself is injured. We do not speak unless necessary. We are a city in mourning.

Across rooftops, I see blackened peaks in all directions, yet I do not understand the full extent of the devastation until I watch it on television and see the images in the paper. Five hundred homes and four lives have been lost. Entire streets gone, two hundred homes in one suburb alone. Countless animals killed. Infrastructure destroyed and the pine plantations levelled. Historic telescopes and buildings at the Mount Stromlo Observatory consumed by the flames.

Over 160,000 hectares of bushland and farmland have been burned; almost seventy percent of the ACT's Green Zone is now black.

*

The Urambi Hills are only a few minutes away from my house on foot. Before the fires, I had taken to walking a winding route around the neighbourhood, partly to orient myself, partly for exercise. The first time I approach the hills after the fire, my eyes water from the acrid smoke lingering in the air. I deviate from my well-trodden path and head up into the hills, charred grass and leaves turning to dust beneath my feet. At the highest point, I see the rolling waves of green have now been replaced by a sea of patchy black. The fire has burned right up to the back fences of the houses, with telltale scorch marks on some, gaping holes in others, but they are the lucky ones. They had been able to stop the flames.

Wild rabbits, their brown fur stark against the charcoaled ground, watch me warily from a distance. I begin bringing bags of carrots into the hills until my husband gently reminds me I can't save them all.

*

Weeks pass. My feet pound the pavement, my gaze focused on the ground. Out of the corner of my eye, an alien landscape catches my attention. I can still recall it now, almost two decades later: a colour so vivid and intense it seemed almost childish, like a toddler had grabbed a texta and slashed it across the page.

On the charred and blackened remains of the hills are now sparks of fluorescent green. New life hums – from the shoots bursting forth from blackened tree trunks to the carpet of vivid new grass.

I take a deep breath and smell the crisp scent of hope. Rain is coming.

Doorways and Hinges—Anna Jacobson

MLS, PSY

I didn't think a PhD was something I could ever do. PhDs were for other people – surely not me. A Doctor of Philosophy? Impossible. But I have a project I want to complete. I have been holding the loose ends of my memoir since I began writing about my hospitalisation from 2011. Maybe a creative practice PhD would help me finish this project.

*

I run the idea of doing a PhD past Psychiatrist. I trust her and believe she cares about me. I have seen her for a long time – nearly a decade. If I ever need to get in touch about a symptom, she will reply to my email or phone call within a few days. She has dark circles under her eyes, which sometimes look permanently bruised by tiredness. She sometimes tells me I am her most creative patient. At the end of every fortnightly session, Psychiatrist opens the door for me as a courtesy and I walk out. I tell Psychiatrist about my idea of doing a PhD as if holding a shifting rainbow, trying to share glimpses of possibility with her – wanting her encouragement.

Are you sure you want to do a PhD? I don't think that's a good idea. My other patients doing PhDs are all in hospital.

The rainbow between my palms vanishes. She doesn't think I can do it – isn't even willing to give me my own chance. She opens the door for me, and I walk out. A door can symbolise transition and metamorphosis, but I start to feel stymied by each appointment. Years ago, I had talked with Psychiatrist about the idea of reducing my medications due to their adverse side effects.

I don't want a repeat of what happened at hospital. These are the meds we have to work with – I know they're not perfect.

I am shut down and silenced. My views are swept away as absurd and not discussed further. She opens the door for me, and I walk out. In dreams, doors can symbolise challenge or rejection, depending on how far they open or close. If a doorway or latch sticks, I become superstitious that things aren't as they should be. Psychiatrist has led me to believe that noncompliance = psychosis = hospitalisation = electroconvulsive therapy (ECT) without consent = memory loss = loss of self = trauma = rebuilding of self over months and years.

I believe I would be risking my sanity by leaving Psychiatrist. I stay with her, thinking I am safeguarding myself against going mad again – unaware I am trapped in a 'therapeutic' relationship that is destroying my attempts at independence. Destruction by compliance.

You are setting yourself up for failure if you work full-time.

*

Despite her discouragement of my PhD path, I find two PhD supervisors who will take me on. My meetings and discussions with my supervisors are everything that my appointments with Psychiatrist are not. I feel respected, encouraged, and enlightened – pushed and extended creatively. I craft my courage by detangling events. I weave a memoir of my madness from 2011 – a complex project. How do I write my memoir with so many memory gaps from ECT and psychosis? My supervisors are excited by my challenge.

*

I start my project a week before the pandemic is declared in 2020. My principal supervisor suggests I explore the field of Narrative Medicine in my research – a field that aims to create conditions for empathy between doctor and patient through storytelling. This leads me to stumble across the field of Mad Studies, which focuses on the lived experiences of psychiatric survivors and the knowledge we hold. I discover psychiatric survivor activism that I did not know existed. The PhD holds me together during the following three years of my candidature.

When Psychiatrist asks me about my PhD, she says she's never heard of Narrative Medicine or Mad Studies. I don't dare use the term 'psychiatric survivor' – current and ex-patients of mental health services who consider themselves survivors from the interventions of psychiatry – in her presence.

Have you had your pinky toes amputated?

No, they just curl under my other toes.

She opens the door for me, and I walk out.

*

When I was three, I found myself in the corridor of my family home. I had come to the realisation that going one way or the other would change the course of my life. My future would be rewritten based on the choice I made, and I couldn't move – my first existential crisis. I walked part way to the kitchen, following the cork floorboards, and then, as if tugged the other way, turned back and retraced my steps towards the family room with its red clay-coloured tiles. Then I stopped again, standing at the corridor where the paths branched from cork floorboards to tiles. I had chosen not to go anywhere. I stood there, not moving, torn between the two paths.

*

I've been Psychiatrist's patient for nearly a decade. I've had the courage to leave psychologists who were not right for me, so why do I find it so hard to leave Psychiatrist? Is it because I think my sanity is at stake? Is it because medication is involved, which can cause serious harm if not managed correctly by Psychiatrist? Would the next psychiatrist be even worse? I draw squares in my notebook, trapped in their geometry, pathways and doors.

How about you put away your notebook?

I have questions I'd like to ask you.

Why don't you put it away? I ask my other patients to put their notebooks away but have never done this with you.

Why not?

I feel you have a low level of tolerability.

What would we do if I didn't ask the questions I needed to?

I don't know. Maybe we would talk more freely.

She opens the door for me, and I walk out. In Roman mythology, Janus is the god of doorways and transitions, but Cardea is the goddess of door hinges and doorknobs. Cardea stops evil spirits from crossing thresholds. She is a goddess of health, changing seasons, and has powers of protection. In my memoir, I choose Cardea as the name for the hinge of my mad self.

Sometimes I imagine the madness lying dormant, ready to erupt into a second episode when I am next unwell, only because of the narrative that Psychiatrist and others in the mental health 'care' system have told me. I need to regain my independence. The constant pressures and fears around my health are holding me back – I am looking over my shoulder for something I cannot see.

I don't have a crystal ball.

The sessions with Psychiatrist are draining and can turn as bitter as a dissolving antidepressant. Psychiatrist can only keep her composure when my health is going smoothly, but I still can't understand she isn't right for me.

I can't just wave a magic wand to make you feel better.

*

At the end of 2020, Psychiatrist tells me I have acute anxiety and need to go into hospital to change over to a different antidepressant.

I may need to put you in community housing.

After I survive my second hospital admission, which is retraumatising, I realise the new antidepressant is causing severe adverse effects. Psychiatrist had continued to push the dose higher before she left on holiday. I know in my gut it's the antidepressant causing me to have suicidal ideation. At the next session,

Psychiatrist reluctantly agrees with me and says I should come off the antidepressant.

*

Have you heard from your family lately? There was a house fire in their suburb this morning.

She opens the door for me, and I walk out. Doorways can cause forgetting known as the 'doorway effect' – forgetfulness from moving between rooms. And yet when I move from Psychiatrist's office to reception to pay for my appointment, my body doesn't forget how it feels.

*

At some point, Psychiatrist gives me an out-of-date book listing every antidepressant on the market. I look at the dizzying list of drugs and their side effects, one of which is 'sudden death'. When I tried to reduce my antidepressant in the past, Psychiatrist believed my underlying condition was returning, rather than it being the side effects of withdrawal. This made me uncertain in myself. Psychiatrists don't often acknowledge or recognise withdrawal symptoms when the time comes to begin tapering off medications. Psychiatrist convinced me to go back on the antidepressant at an even higher dose than before I'd started the taper.

*

Not one doctor has ever acknowledged the harm and trauma caused by my first involuntary hospitalisation, the fallout from the forced ECT treatments and the continuing medication regime for a diagnosis that is in dispute after a second opinion from another psychiatrist.

Try not to attack those who are trying to help you.

She opens the door for me, and I walk out. In 2011, the heavy hospital ward door slammed on my finger when I tried to escape. The scar in the shape of a fishing hook remains.

*

I don't pick an antidepressant from the out-of-date book. I return it to Psychiatrist two weeks after she handed it to me. She appears surprised she provided me the book in the first place and looks at me like I am lying that she ever gave me the choice from the antidepressant roulette wheel.

She tells me again: *I don't want a repeat of what happened at your first hospitalisation.*

I'm on an antipsychotic now, remember?

Your antipsychotic is already at a low dose.

I cry with frustration, anger and hopelessness. My antipsychotic dose has not been lowered since I'd left hospital in 2011. I am also crying with something else – grief.

I'm thinking of making our appointments once every three months instead of fortnightly.

That's ridiculous, Anna. How can I properly monitor you if I only see you once every three months?

I know in my gut that instead of fewer appointments with Psychiatrist, I need to take a risk and change psychiatrists altogether. I am being over-monitored. Over-medicated. But I still believe I am risking my sanity by leaving her. After all, I haven't had another period of madness since 2011. What if this is because of Psychiatrist's guidance? Or is it despite having her as my psychiatrist? Still, I believe that leaving Psychiatrist = psychosis = hospitalisation = ECT without consent = memory loss = loss of self = trauma = rebuilding of self over months and years.

I've been on this journey with you for nine years.

No, you haven't. You may have been paid for forty-five-minute sessions every two weeks, but you have not lived my experience, felt my emotions. To claim this is an insult.

I do not say these words, only stare at the floor, tears leaking.

What's the best thing in your life?

My family and friends.

And the worst?

She drags out the silence and when I move to speak, she cuts me off.

Your health, she says, putting words in my mouth. Her eyes become shadowy, and she looks at me like I'm dying.

The mental health 'care' system is the worst thing in my life, though I feel unsafe uttering these words in her office. I continue to remain silent.

Try to stay in the present. We'll leave it there for today.

For the first time in nine years, she doesn't open the door for me. Sometimes the smallest act, after a long time of being stuck, can set a person free. Her not opening the door is my reason to change. A decade's worth of her remarks whiplash through my head.

You have a face that's hard to read – some would call it 'resting bitch face' – you should practise smiling in the mirror.

Your attitude needs fixing.

If you find driving stressful, why bother?

I seem to have pushed your buttons – touched a nerve.

Do you feel normal?

Her not opening the door enables me to make the most courageous act I have ever taken in a medical space where I felt I had no voice. I open the door, let myself out, and never go back.

*

My writing and art is an act of courage out of necessity and passion for creating. Leaving Psychiatrist took a different kind of courage. I thought my sanity depended on staying with her. I have needed courage to stand up to those in control of my care. Courage to seek out another psychiatrist. Despite all the harmful interventions the mental health 'care' system has zapped, over-medicated and slammed through my brain and central nervous system, I am still here. My courage is a fiery light that may dim at times but never extinguishes, roaring into a beacon when it needs to.

*

My GP encourages me to send an email to Psychiatrist to let her know I am not returning to her practice. I write the words a psychologist once said to me: I feel we are no longer the right fit. Psychiatrist replies that my intelligence and creative talent have stood out to her even when my mental health has been challenging for me. She hopes I continue to draw on this as I take a new direction. She wishes me the best with my health, career and life.

I am now free from a qualified professional who discouraged me from doing a PhD, and driving, and who said I would be setting myself up for failure if I ever tried full-time work. I never knew which version of Psychiatrist I would get – the version who told me I was her most creative patient, or the version who didn't seem to realise the harm her comments exuded with each interaction. Psychiatrist may have made notes on me over nine years, but now the tables and chairs have flipped. I am speaking back to my experience.

Writing these words has been empowering. An act of courage. I complete my memoir and submit my PhD. I am nominated by both my external examiners for the Outstanding Doctoral Thesis Award. The support from my supervisors and mentors, learning about other psychiatric survivors and researchers in Mad Studies, and my own writing get me through a difficult time. I graduate. I slowly reduce my dose with another psychiatrist, so that I am no longer as sedated by my medication. I do well in my new full-time contract job. I thrive when being busy. I receive a publishing offer from NewSouth for my memoir, *How to Knit a Human*. I am a woman of a certain courage, surrounded by many others of a certain courage. May our stories help others feel less alone. May we find the courage to leave, when we need to. May our courage be enacted over again, in our own fiery way, on our own terms, always.

Learning to Swim—Eliora Avrahami

CA, MI, SA

1.
I was a water baby, that's what my parents called me. Like a lot of people in Perth, I grew up spending my summers at the beach, swimming in our backyard pool, and at swimming carnivals at school. But that doesn't mean I have always known how to really swim, to trust in the ability of my body to keep me safe in the depths, to find the resolve to keep moving my arms and kicking my legs. That took much, much longer.

2.
It has long passed from science to common sense that life began in the ocean, that it first pulled itself out of the shallows. As the science writer Rachel Carson has noted, the shore unsettles us even in its undeniable beauty, and ever since God divided land from water at the beginning of Genesis our oldest stories have told us of our fears, and desires, of the ocean.[1] We began in the sea, and return to it uneasily, afraid of what lurks beneath.

3.
When I was in primary school, we spent two weeks every summer at the beach, five days a week, from eight until noon when the Indian Ocean swells became too strong for my sister and me.

My mother taught for the Education Department's summer swimming program, wearing a fluoro yellow bib to be noticeable to her young charges through the breakers. I remember distinctly her showing me how to bend my elbow for freestyle, and how to do a frog kick for breaststroke; and me trying and failing to do butterfly. My sister was much more proficient than I was, going on to get her Bronze Medallion and become a swimming teacher herself when she studied at university, but I still managed to make my way through most of the stages, gaining a certificate for my efforts most summers. My father was with us, but mostly stayed on the beach, having never really learned how to master his fear of the ocean. I remember sandwiches for lunch, or fish and chips and Kirks Kolé Beer from the nearby kiosk if we were lucky, but mostly what I remember is the taste of salt and sand whenever the waves dumped me, the sense of disorientation, the fear where you become unsure of what way is up or down, which way to swim towards the air.

4.

Philosopher Luce Irigaray says that water in itself is gendered feminine to the earth's masculine in our culture. Think about the things sailors say about the ocean – untrustworthy, capricious, quicksilver. Irigaray says, especially for men, that the eternal flux of liquid means that culturally speaking, there are few places that hold more peril than the sea.[2] The very language we use to describe materiality privileges solid over liquid, land over sea. Or to put it another: you have to treat the ocean like a lover, some say, or she will drown you.

But what if you treat your lovers like the ocean, if you are unsure of the constancy of their love, fearing it will swallow you in a wave and deposit you spluttering on the shore? How do you find the courage to trust when you have learned not to rely on other people?

5.
In the kitchen a few weeks ago, I was doing dishes and listening to Sade, my hands deep in soapy water, when I began to dissociate. I felt the familiar pull as my sense of self left; I saw but did not feel. I wiped my hands clean, turned off the bluetooth speaker, walked in a daze to the lounge room and told my wife, 'You need to put me to bed.' She made the bed for me, rearranged the blankets, handed me the teddy bear my trauma-informed psychologist had recommended I buy and sat beside me to sing soft lullabies. The world was haze and my body a great distance away, but I felt involuntarily turned on, and I told my wife this, a fact that filled me with shame the next day when I returned. 'You know why that is,' I said to her, and she said, 'There are many reasons, but you are safe now,' and she stroked my hair until I fell asleep.

6.
In his wonderful little book *In Praise of Love*,[3] philosopher Alain Badiou talks about the need to reinvent love for the present day. He talks about the evolution of a 'safety first' ethos of love in the present day that impoverishes our experience of love, that we think about emotional connection in the same way as we might purchase an insurance policy or investment. We might think that we can buy love, on Tinder or Grindr, or rent it, but these are the illusions of a world where everything is for sale but the essential.

In the age of dating apps, sex is readily available, to be sure. Yet it comes with a cost: it's hard to think of a more effective method of dehumanisation than the movement from person to virtual avatar. Reducing attraction to a swift evaluation then a swipe is not only alienating in the abstract sense, in that it demeans the human dignity of the other person, but also self-alienating in removing the user from an authentic, unmediated relationship to their own sexual desire. Where in the early twentieth century, Freudian-influenced writers like D.H. Lawrence could imagine an oceanic sexuality lying underneath the repression of civilisation, now there is precious little space for desire outside of the commodification of sexuality.

Reading Badiou I think: safety first, courage last?

7.
So where does that leave love? Can we still speak of love in this heartless epoch, where everyone is called to be as self-sufficient – self-contained – as possible and every form of care is increasingly denigrated? What space is left for the vulnerability of another person, for weakness, for desire? When love is a commodity traded on the open market of the internet, it sometimes seems like there is no such thing as 'falling' in love anymore – love is a product purchased by the app consumer, and if you prove a bad investment, flawed in any way, your partner will simply move on to a better option.

8.
And yet, I did fall in love with someone, and online to boot. I met her on the open seas of Twitter, back when it was still called that, sailing into her inbox and her life. When we were newly in love, we would sing each other a song by the indie-pop band The Submarines called 'Swimming Pool', about the recklessness of love and water. My new lover was decidedly not a water baby,

having grown up on an inland sheep farm hundreds of kilometres from the coast. What she was, and is, is solid like the earth, and that year she dragged me from the rising tide by the heartstrings.

9.
At those childhood swimming lessons, I learned how to do CPR, lest I ever encounter someone unconscious in the swell. In those days, CPR meant starting with three quick breaths, then three chest compressions to each breath, but now the Australian Resuscitation Council recommends thirty compressions to every two breaths, recognising the importance of keeping the heart going.

'Courage', of course, comes from the Latin *cor*, meaning heart.

10.
When I had newly moved to Victoria to be with my love, the two of us and her five-year-old daughter went to a beach in sheltered Port Phillip Bay. Neither she nor my new stepdaughter were particularly comfortable in the water, and I had long lost any skill I had attained in childhood. Instead, we splashed around happily in the shallows, until one of Melbourne's famed 'changes' – here they just call it 'The Change' in summer – came in giant gusts of wind, blowing us from the shore in swirls of sand around our ankles back to my wife's Corolla. It was the first time I had witnessed such a dramatic transformation, the power of weather to change a pleasant afternoon into a fight for comfort and banishment from the elements.

11.
The thing that preoccupies Badiou is not simply falling in love but *staying* in love – love as a 'tenacious adventure'.[4] How do you stay in love across the years, not when things are fresh and new, but on the boring Mondays, the nights in front of the television, through sickness and health? And what do you do when you find it hard to trust in the power of your own strokes through the sea?

12.
When I was six, I went for a swim with my grandfather at Cottesloe Beach, I think, though it might have been Trigg, and afterwards, we got changed in the toilet block/changing room. There are things I can tell you about that day: my grandfather's swimming trunks were tan, my bathers were red and gold, the tiles were brown, there was a drip of water from the roof. I can also tell you that before I was born, my grandfather went to jail for molesting three boys, and my parents left me alone with him a decade later. There are other things I can't tell directly, not even after years of therapy, though you can probably guess what they are.

13.
While Badiou is more or less right about capitalism, we might see love as being under threat from other broader systems, too, like patriarchy and heterosexism (two things French philosophers like Badiou tend to spend little time thinking about). Love is under threat from the patriarchs, little and big, who abuse their power, who make us distrust ourselves and flinch before the blow. It's under threat from the institutions that take the shapes of bodies that don't look like yours, made for the privilege and comfort of people who do not look or sound or love like you.

It's easy to adopt a 'safety first' attitude when you have been hurt before, and neglected by the people supposed to take care of you.

So it's understandable that you might not want to swim in the deepest part of the ocean, that you might need floaties or a surfboard or someone to keep you afloat. You might fear the face of the deep, the way that monsters lurk beyond the shallows. According to the midrash, holy Jewish writings on the Bible, Noah spent 120 years preparing his ark of safety, but you don't have that long. So when you go to the beach, you might think that if you swim between the flags, you will stay safe, but you would be wrong, and that is the dread and the wonder of it.

14.
Shame is corrosive, and it eats away at every part of you, twisting your stomach into knots and your heart into a dead weight in the very pith of you. My psychologist says that children blame themselves, that it is easier to see the way you are treated as something you somehow deserve than to pass judgement on the adults you trust. For most of my life I have thought that it happened because I was too feminine, too pretty and too queer, rather than the simple fact that I was there, like all of the others. It is easier to turn the hatred inside than out. It is easier to surrender to the surf than keep treading water.

15.
Twenty years after I first told a lover, in the vaguest of terms, what had happened to me, my friend and I were eating Japanese food at an otherwise empty city restaurant when we saw a homeless man looking at us through the window, with his hands in his pants moving back and forth, and between that and

another incident of sexual harassment soon after at work, in the weeks following I felt unmoored from my life. I floated out to sea, far away from the woman I love and the child I care for, my strokes lacking any power, swallowing salt water and beginning to drown.

My wife took two weeks off work to take care of me, driving me to see my rabbi who I told that I was suicidal, that I felt so afraid that I couldn't go on any longer. I said that I am afraid of climate change, of raging bushfires and storm fronts sweeping the coastline, that I cannot see a future for myself in this world. This was true, but it was only half the truth – the truth is that I was and am deathly afraid of being loved, of losing love, of having love. I was afraid of the steadiness I see in my wife's eyes, of digging deep into relation with a single person, of fucking and fighting and making up and working and gathering around our table, night after night and year after year. I had my life, everything I have ever wanted, and in the wake of indecent exposure, I began to lack the strength to hold onto it.

16.

It took a year of intense therapy to bring me back, to get me to the point where I could trust in the constancy of her fidelity, our shared faithfulness to the event of our love. I was lucky enough to find someone who, despite it all, continues to want my kisses and snuggles on the couch, who has pulled me through a year of depression with every determined stroke of her arms. I hope – intend – to swim towards her for the rest of my life, to meet every new incarnation of her just as she meets every new version of me, to bask in the sun as the light hits the waves, glittering and glimmering. I hope to watch the sun set over the coast, to eat fish and chips and gelato at the shore, to feel the breeze brisk against my skin and see the horizon in the distance, to lean against my lover and feel the embrace of sure feeling.

17.
Several weeks ago, after spending most of the year in the darkest of clouds, I talked to my rabbi again, telling her that I wanted to go to the *mikveh*, the Jewish ritual bath used to mark conversions, marriages, fertility and other significant moments. I told her, through tears, as simply as I could, that I wanted to be clean, I wanted the water to wash away the dirt of the past from my body. I told her that I wanted to be present, and strong, and whole. She told me she understood, and that she had worked with women before who had used the mikveh to heal, and that we would create something meaningful together. Later, she texted me, and said, *chazak v'amatz* – strength and courage.

18.
So here I am, ready to immerse myself. Ready to let go of the past, all of the fear and pain and shame, to find the bravery to accept love as well as give it.

To learn, once again, how to swim.

Resistance as Courage—Sally Scott

MLS, SH

In his 1894 novel *Pudd'nhead Wilson*, Mark Twain reflects that 'Courage is resistance to fear, mastery of fear – not an absence of fear.'[1] I cannot imagine a life that does not have fear. I can imagine a life that has had too much fear and the exhaustion of resistance, because I have lived that life. Writing this is an exercise in fear and self-doubt – fear that people will respond with dislike of me as the subject; self-doubt that I can write about something that reflects my reality. Is my life one that demonstrates the qualities of resilience, bravery and fearlessness that are often associated with courage? In writing this piece can I take ownership of the word 'courage' to describe my progress through the months and years of cancer and mental illness?

These questions may not be answered. They may be left hanging – left up to the reader to decide.

My first experience of a deep and unsettling fear was when I lived with my family in Zeehan in Tasmania's north-west. A town without a heart, it housed miners who left and were replaced in a rapid cycle that curtailed connections. It was an ever-changing loose gathering of souls.

On a rare hot summer's day, our little family went to nearby Queenstown to swim in its new pool. I was six and in a continual struggle to maintain a presence squashed between two extroverted brothers. On reflection, Queenie seems like an ageing harlot whose buildings looked like a greying bit of lace encircling the denuded thigh of Mount Lyle. She was quixotic as men used her resources, leaving her bereft of her wealth. She served only to relinquish.

The pool on that day was full of pasty bodies exposed to twenty-four degrees and a sky unblemished by clouds. This was our only visit to the pool that I can remember. At first I stayed down the shallow end, keeping my shoulders and head clear of the water. Then, gripping the side of the pool, I edged myself along, feeling exhilaration at my audacity to go into a depth that was over my head.

Then I lost my grip and my body jerked backwards. I sank. Bobbing up, I tried to reach the edge, but it was beyond my fingertips. I sank again, swallowing water that hit the back of my throat and made me gag. I bobbed up again. The side was further away. Even now I do not know how I made it back to the side of the pool to cling on while I vomited. I climbed out and vomited again, the water splashing onto the paving. The fear and shame made me cry. I went to my mother.

'What are you sooking for?'

'Nothing.'

I sat on my towel and pulled my knees tightly to my chest, wanting to be as small as possible.

'We didn't come this far for you to just sit on your towel. Go and swim.'

But I couldn't swim. I could only drown.

Terrified, I got back into the water and, turning on the spot, I created eddies whose slow, consistent circles calmed me. The fear did not stop, but it abated with each circle that quietly rolled away. Was that fearful little girl showing the first spark of courage?

Dear Sally,

Swimming will become a frightening thing for the rest of your life. And you will never forget the fear of drowning. The smell of the chlorine, the sounds of people around you who are unaware of your distress and the feel of the water in your throat will stay with you. You will never swim at the beach but merely splash in the shallows and watch other people as they boldly go out into the depths. You will visualise them drowning and the lifesavers running out to rescue them. Then you will admonish yourself for being paranoid. Your fear is your own and thinking through it is your method of resistance.

Much love, Sally

Now in my fifties, I have the privilege of looking back and mapping my fears like a cartographer maps topography.

In my mid-twenties I was diagnosed with bipolar – only just missing the old nomenclature of manic depression. But the language didn't make a difference because no name could represent the glorious elevations and the frightening plunges. The up and down that defines my understanding of everything I do.

Then at fifty-two I was diagnosed with breast cancer, and my fears about that unruly breast compounded the daily fear that is living with bipolar.

Which fear is greater? Which requires the greater resistance?

Cancer is a strange word. Its first three letters I see as positives, as in 'can do', 'can be', and the second three are neutral. On first hearing the diagnosis, I wasn't fearful; rather, I was distracted by the concept of cancer as belonging to other people. And it wasn't until I saw my surgeon and my mammogram that I understood that this cancer belonged to me. Then my fear was less about the tumour and more about my lack of control. As Julia Baird says in *Phosphorescence*, 'It's a peculiar, lonely kind of impotence, a cancer diagnosis. Even if you ran a thousand miles, aced a billion exams or hit a dozen home runs, nothing could reverse or erase the fact of cancer.'[2]

Control is given over to surgeons, oncologists and nurses, and it is an act of faith just to turn up. To resist the fear that says, 'I hope they know what they're doing' takes enormous energy and belief. Belief in the people around you, but also belief in the drugs they administer. I didn't want to question the efficacy of the chemotherapy drugs because having numbers about rates of success simply increases the fear: will I be in the eighty percent that respond, or that other group? To manage my fears I became passive – doing whatever the nurses told me to do on the days that I got 'plugged in'. I listened to the oncologist and didn't question her treatment plan. When I developed a blood clot, I listened to the haematologist and injected myself every day to try to dissolve it. But there was resistance in that passivity: the more I listened, the stronger I became; the more I noticed the efficacy of the treatment, the more I was able to control my fears. I couldn't control the cancer, but I could manage my response. And it changed from fear to acceptance, through passivity to agency.

Dear Sally,

Cancer will test your resolve as you work hard to feel normal and fearless. You tell yourself you are not ill, it's simply a glitch in the machine to be worked on by the mechanics of drug therapies administered by nurses who will treat you with kindness and respect. Elements that facilitate your belief in an end date that will see your hair grow back and blunt your memory of the worst moments. They will help build

your resistance to a fear of death and ameliorate your sense of being out of control. You will be your own mistress.
Much love, Sally

Bipolar is ferocious. Part of the plan for my cancer was an end date – the point at which I would be told that I was a survivor. The end date for bipolar is death.

I don't fear that end, rather I fear the time in between – the struggle to maintain normalcy between a brain that wants to make grandiose plans for all the things it has made me buy at Bunnings and the brain that ceases to understand the simplest things. One that is paranoid and agitated and can only be calmed by self-mutilation.

That is the brain that a line of psychiatrists has tried to control with an ever-changing combination of chemicals. There will be no end point for the mix of seven tablets I take to keep me from experiencing a mind that seeks to self-immolate. I was confident that chemotherapy would resolve the cancer, I am not confident that my psychotropics will control my bipolar. I live with the fear that my mind will explode and that I will become a non-person – a being that breathes, walks and perceives the world, but cannot speak for fear of shattering.

My fears live a vibrant life within my home. Utensils must point the same way – they are checked every morning and throughout the day, as though some mysterious force will come and mix them up. I fear that they are out of place, just as I fear that the contents of my pantry are no longer arranged in alphabetical order, or that the remote controls are not in a straight line. I am a watcher of things.

The drugs for cancer were controlled by an oncologist and administered by nurses every Thursday. They had a definiteness, a shape, that my bipolar medications do not, for they rely on the inexact science of psychiatry and on me to administer them. Why, when I am high, do I need drugs? And when I am in a mixed state of both confusion and detachment, why do I deserve drugs? The enforced compliance of cancer therapy becomes contingent for bipolar therapies. I fear the paranoia that tells me big pharma wants to keep me ill, therefore I shouldn't passively take medication that contributes to an industry that wants people to be sick. Wellness is anathema to its business model. Most of the time I can resist this fear, but there are times it overwhelms me – my courage fails and I am put into a clinic where new, temporary medications sedate me, keeping me safe from myself. Slowly my resistance builds, and I am let out to again start the process of being normal.

My cancer was visible. My bald head signified the treatment that was blasting the vestiges of cancer to smithereens. I could see the sympathy in the faces of people as I walked around assuming my normal life, as they acknowledged the baldness, the sallow skin and the dark rings under my eyes. People accepted my cancer – it was bad, they didn't ever want the experience, but they could have empathy for the struggle.

My bipolar is invisible. On the rare occasions when I have disclosed it, the response has often been, 'But you look normal.' So what does bipolar look like? For me, the physical manifestations are obvious. They are the bags of new things that I gather on a spending binge at the shopping centre. They are the talking excitably about mundane things. They are the lack of sleep because, who needs sleep when you're invincible? They are the shaking hands because you've stopped taking your medication. It is a magnificent fearlessness.

But then, it is also an elision of family and friends, of familiar routines and a state of rest. It is an irreversible sadness that rapidly degenerates into paranoia and the cutting of flesh. The latter being the only visible manifestation of a state of mind that seeks the destruction of the host. Disordered thinking is the label, and the cure is a temporary fix of chemicals that sedate and nauseate. My resilience is lost in a fog. It is an absolute fearfulness.

Higher doses of medication begin to work. For those close enough to see, my resolve starts to assert itself. My behaviours begin to resemble the normal me. It becomes a match between that part of my brain which has given in to the bipolar and that other part of my brain which now seeks to assert itself. To push away the fear and resolve to begin the process of becoming myself. Looking in the mirror, I can see a different me. I become substantial again, with the capacity to think and reflect, to connect and to control. It is a moment of clarity where I see the bipolar as an external illness much like my cancer, with all its visible side effects.

Dear Sally,

It will always happen, those boom-and-bust cycles and the fear they elicit. You will be exhausted and the desire for obliteration will be strong. The strongest thing you will ever feel. But then people gather: nurses, a psychiatrist, a psychologist and a husband who know the temporality of this chemical paralysis. They will be kind and respectful, and they will empathise with your state as they seek to help you out of it. Gradually you will feel that your heart pumps as it should, and you will notice things outside your window – the hibiscus, the cars parked higgledy-piggledy at the workplace next door, the people flowing in and out of offices. Your resistance will strengthen and in its wake, fear will disperse.

With my best wishes, Sally

The coming home from cancer treatment is a moment of deep comfort. Walking into the house, smelling its smell and hearing its sounds brings a calmness that nurtures and replenishes. Home is what I think about as I am plugged in and watching the quiet busyness of the ward. I look forward to it as a peaceful space where I can reimagine myself as the well woman I was before that three-minute phone call that rocked my world. Home is a husband who has his own fears that I can see every time he looks at my baldness. I want to allay them as I allay my own. Home gives me the strength to look fear straight on and diminish it.

Coming home from the psychiatric clinic is a moment of discombobulation. Here is the space where I am at my sickest, yet also at my most well. Where I am at my most fearful but also at my most resilient. Where most of my paranoia has free rein, yet where I have the greatest clarity. Bipolar makes my home both a retreat and a prison where I am obsessed by minutiae that keeps me out of my social circle – cutlery, containers of flour and sugar and the order of condiments in my fridge become my focus. The outside world ceases to exist and my mind is smashed by a cacophony of noisy voices that block reason. My only clear thoughts are of annihilation.

But when I get home, that same calmness that allows my cancer-self to breathe allows my bipolar self to begin the process of resistance. It becomes a resistance to a mind that seeks to succumb to the fearful excess of the disease. With every day, I can wake and feel the surges of self-belief that will be my ballast. I gingerly start to return to the world of people where I talk as though nothing has happened to interrupt my story. As with cancer, I seek to reassure people that I am resisting the temptation to fold up, to disappear from view until the medications have done their job.

Fear has never been absent from my life. It has waxed and waned but has never left me; it has never given me the space to console myself. Instead, I try to suspend its excesses, distract myself by experiencing my daily existence moment by moment. Slowing time down to its most rudimentary. This allows a stillness that coalesces with fear. Baird uses the Ngan'gikurunggurr word for deep listening, *dadirri*, to describe this state of being still.[3] I have learned that this quiet can coexist with fear – suppressing it to something momentarily manageable. But it is of the moment. All I can do is seek to string these suspensions of time into ever greater lengths because I want to be present. I want to have mastery over all my fears, rational and otherwise. I *need* to resist fear to make these things happen. Resistance as Mark Twain expresses it suggests that fear is a marker of our humanity and that to resist is part of the human condition.

But is this resistance also a marker of courage?

Have Courage, Dear Heart—Shel Sweeney

Women in patriarchal societies are, by nature, courageous – it takes courage to thrive in a society that has, historically and presently, tried to control women. Often in Western societies, stereotypically masculine traits (strength, assertiveness and singular focus) are held in high esteem, and stereotypically feminine traits such as intuition, connection and self-awareness are seen as lesser in some way. Western women, however, are being called on to work harder longer, to compartmentalise and to set aside their emotional world in order to be seen as equal to their male counterparts, all the while, often, being paid less for their troubles. It is a brave woman who decides this way of being does not work for her. Have courage, dear hearts.[1] What do you need? Courage is our capacity to feel fear but to take whatever action is necessary anyway. It takes courage for a woman to live her life on her terms, consequences be damned. Courage orients us toward our growing edge, that place of discomfort that can, at times, feel razor-sharp dangerous.

Have courage, dear heart, I have learned to say to myself. *What do I need?* This is the foundation of my wellspring of fierce fortitude. It is my courage to put all else aside, listen deeply to the self and ensure, as they say on planes, that my air mask is firmly in place before I assist others. This means that I recognise and give voice to the terms I want to live my life by, even when that is against the grain, and I take the necessary steps that lead me in this direction. And what direction is this? One that is deeply aligned to my values and to my sense of connection and interconnectedness.

This is not always a popular stance. There is a particular narrative, stretching back through time, that has been imposed upon women's bodies, women's rights, women's voices, women's stories and women's lives by others – often male-dominated structures, organisations and, sometimes, individuals. I reflect on the acquisition and development of my own courage. I was a shy child, but I had great role models. My mum took the lead in moving the family from poverty on the other side of the world to Australia, where she hoped for better opportunities for her children, and my father retrained as a social worker after years of working in the male-dominated construction industry.

I found new ways of being in the books I read, like Angela Carter's *The Bloody Chamber*, a feminist reworking of fairytales; singers I listened to – PJ Harvey and Sinéad O'Connor, thriving in a male-dominated industry; designers like Vivienne Westwood, redefining fashion; the feminist group Guerilla Girls, fighting sexism in the art world; and so many more. Then I had a child, and I knew that courage also meant having the courage to love, the courage to stand in my conviction, the courage to admit when things were not going well or when I was wrong, and the courage to change things not just for one's own sake but for the sake of others. My own experience and a desire to impact the world with positive change for my child and for others coming after me became motivating factors to do the work I do as a counsellor and editor. I hoped to help those struggling to find their own selves and their own courage in circumstances and situations that may have other ideas for them. Legal and medical systems and government policies still control women's rights to a range of freedoms.

Courageous women have been and still are brought into line in a number of overt and subtle ways. 'You are so perceptive,' I am told – but read between the lines and you will hear that I am 'too sensitive', 'too emotional', 'too unstable' – like many women before me deemed hysterical, I am 'unpalatable'. 'You have such good boundaries,' I am told – but the unspoken line is that I am too inflexible and not easily manipulated. Like centuries of women before me, I am meant to be available to meet the needs of others. 'You are so clear in your communication,' I am told – the silence that follows speaks of my truth-telling and my honesty.

*

After the 2022 floods in Lismore in the Northern Rivers region of New South Wales, in which I lost two-thirds of all my belongings and the office I had just set up for my own business, I felt the pull of expectation to be there for my community. I'm a writer, editor, counsellor/therapist, teacher, artist … and a woman. The expectation to care that a woman is subjected to by society begins in childhood when we are praised for cradling our baby dolls.

In February 2022, the community of Lismore was decimated, and not just Lismore, many towns and communities up and down the east coast of Australia were inundated by floodwaters. People lost lives, livestock, buildings, homes, everything. Lismore's town centre went underwater; the stuff of every day was swept away. The bodies of cows from the hinterland washed toward the mouth of the Richmond River at Ballina and out to sea. Everything shut down … roads disappeared and communications failed in the wake of telecommunications towers and fibre-optic cables being washed away by floodwaters and landslides.

The Wilson River flows all the way from its beginnings as Upper Wilson Creek, and is joined by Opossum Creek, Stony Creek, Byron Creek, Pearces Creek and Coopers Creek. In Lismore, Leycester Creek (a river in itself really), which begins in the Border Ranges as water gathering through Dreadnought Gully and is fed by Jerrys Creek, Websters Creek, Back Creek and Terania Creek, flows into the Wilson River. Once conjoined, these waters flow together to the Richmond River, which then continues all the way to the ocean. Beginning in mountainous rainforest country, these waterways gathered momentum during the 2022 floods.

The rain gauges in Lismore were damaged by the raging floodwaters, but five kilometres to the west, 861 millimetres was recorded in Tuncester. In town, floodwaters reached 14.4 metres, well into the second floors of many buildings, and into the roof spaces beyond this in some. Lismore City Council's *Impacts & Recovery Statement* estimated that 3,170 Lismore businesses were impacted by the flood, affecting 18,000 workers across the area.[2] But statistics don't tell us what it was like to live with these losses. They don't tell of women and their children tied to light poles in kayaks in the darkness in the middle of the torrent, a gushing river where once their road had stretched a slow path through the houses. They don't tell of the elderly man standing atop a stepladder chest-high in darkness as the river broke in through doors and windows, carrying unnamed things and creatures through his top bedroom as he tried to hold his dog, terror in its eyes, aloft. They don't tell of the horror of watching people on Facebook and Instagram sending out desperate pleas for rescue as waters rose and then as they went silent on socials and we, isolated, were left wondering if they survived. They don't tell of the guilt of locals not flood-affected or who deemed themselves as not flood-affected enough to be worthy of assistance, but who struggled nonetheless. They don't tell of a man with an abscess on his leg where something in the floodwater bit him as he tried to salvage what was left of his life, or the woman struggling with asthma and poor mobility who tried to save her birds while her infirm and hospitalised husband was evacuated to higher ground. I wonder how many litres of tears have been cried through and after the floods, how many litres of tears are still being cried, how many rivers these tears could fill.

I was in shock. The community was in shock. My own experience of the floods included trying to keep safe my dad with Alzheimer's, my mum with lung-and-heart issues and their very anxious dog, then losing almost all I owned at work and at home. It left me on the verge of hopelessness. Everywhere was covered in muddy brown silt, and many out-of-place items teetered where the floodwaters had deposited them: a truck on a boulder in the middle of a river, a washing machine halfway up a tall tree in the crook of a branch, the remains of a community hall scattered through a paddock miles from its original position, sheets of plastic flapping from the underside of a high bridge ... the list goes on. The smell of damp and mould spread from the ground, from walls, from furniture – spores roaming wild and free in the very humid air. We couldn't drink the tap water; the water treatment plant had been compromised by floodwaters carrying sewage and the bodies of dead animals. The Wilson River, Leycester Creek and the Richmond River smelled and were devoid of oxygen.

I felt drained of oxygen, like a fish struggling in an earth-sodden river. Had it not been for supportive family and friends, I'm not sure how I would have coped in those first weeks. I had never been afraid of rain before, and the rain continued. The sound of each drop felt like a threat, like I might die. It emptied me out. Pieces of me washed away. I was drowning, though the floodwaters were receding. I moved in and out of fight, flight and freeze responses, sometimes all three in rapid succession. My nervous system was so heightened that I was barely functioning. That first week after the floods I spent sorting through my sodden life, throwing things out, cleaning what could be salvaged and trying, in ninety-seven percent humidity, to dry things out. I felt numb much of the time and panicked the rest.

*

I remember, weeks later, finally feeling able to start exercising again, finally being able to go outside and take a walk. I went to my favourite bush path along the coastal sand dunes, a place where I had always felt connected to nature, expansive of heart and grounded and calm, only to discover the pathway still flooded. I burst into tears, chest pounding, palms sweaty, and bolted for the car, throwing myself into the driver's seat and taking a good ten minutes to calm my breathing and heart rate. I didn't walk again for another month, but it took much longer to walk in a calm state and find enjoyment in the walking. One of my calming tools had previously been to listen to meditation tracks. It wasn't until after the floods that I realised many of these tracks had nature and rain-based sound effects. Nature was no longer my safe place. These meditation tracks, instead of slowing my breathing and helping me become immersed in deepest peace, only escalated my feelings of danger and panic.

I was working, at the time, a few days a week from a doctor's surgery. So many clients had been flood-impacted and were in varying states of distress and/or ill health. The doctor saw lots of people with wounds and skin problems from being immersed or partially immersed in tainted floodwaters or from having had no access to clean water; then, as the mould spored they began to have chest and breathing problems. A lot of my clients were telling me their stories and I would often need to leave the room because I felt myself drawn in too closely to their trauma, too easily thrown off-centre by my own experience, too pulled into an eddy of panic and fear and weird guilt and shame that came from comparing my story to theirs and from holding myself and my capacity to assist others to a higher level of expectation to assist than I was capable of at the time.

Have courage, dear heart. What do I need? I could not work as a counsellor. I didn't know if I would ever be able to again. I felt broken, like some essential part of myself had been irreparably shattered. I needed courage to step back. I needed to give myself time. I needed to heal. I needed to put on my own air mask.

For six months, I engaged in expressive art as my therapy. I wove baskets – many, many baskets! The natural materials connected me to nature in a safe way. The rhythmic movement of the weaving helped me regulate my breathing and heart rate. I made needle-felted eggs containing crystals, herbs, flowers, feathers – tiny things that connected me to a sense of something larger than myself and yet something small and containable. The sound of the needle moving in and out of the wool was like the crunching of feet on sand and I visualised the beach in happier days: pristine sand, wide blue skies, deep clear ocean and warm sunshine – not a cloud in sight. The engagement of my hands through these simple activities gave my anxieties a direction and focus.

I had been a keeper of diaries and journals and the writer of stories and poems all my life, but now I had no words. There were no words to describe my state of being, to explain what I had experienced or to name what I was going through. I needed a different kind of language, one that would help me move my experiences through my body and psyche somehow. I drew and painted, my inner world expressing itself in colour, line and shape – sometimes showing me something I hadn't known, sometimes nonsensical, but always, always calming and satisfying, leaving me with a feeling of being strongly connected to myself and of having engaged with some kind of medicine. It was meditative, personal, moving and deeply healing. *Have courage, dear heart. What do I need?* While others rebuilt the community, I rebuilt myself. I withdrew and I sang, I danced, I created. And slowly, slowly, I began to emerge again, to engage again with friends, with nature and with my community.

The new me that emerged has learned a thing or two about loss and grief and the courage it takes to face these things in real and meaningful ways: I have learned about boundaries – the boundaries I need to create around myself and my time and my energy; I have found ways that suit me and my needs and my experience, and I have developed the courage to stand in these new ways of being in powerful and dynamic ways. I have learned that the greatest courage I have is the courage to say to myself: *Have courage, dear heart.* To ask: *What do I need?* To really listen to the answer that comes, and then to act upon this answer with the whole of my being, even when the answer at first sounds implausible, unrealistic, inconvenient or impossible – to acknowledge and accept what arises even when what rises up is uncomfortable … this is true courage, this is who I am now, this is my new strength.

*

The 2022 floods pushed me to an edge within myself. For a while, I balanced precariously there – and it was as uncomfortable as any growing edge could be. But I felt my way, and I learned to find small comforts and rest in the turmoil so that soon I began to have the wherewithal to dip my toes over the edge, to feel the water there, then sink my body slowly into its depths, to duck my head beneath its surface, to open my eyes and look for what it held for me. A growing edge – that place of discomfort beyond which, if we can take that courageous step forward, we find new knowledge and wisdom. A growing edge can feel dangerous, like stepping off a cliff edge, crawling through a tight crevice, diving into dark depths – it can feel like we might die. Growing edges are where our sense of self, of reality, of perception is challenged. A growing edge, if we are courageous, is where our vulnerabilities emerge and, if we arm ourselves with compassionate bravery, we learn and change and are consequently expanded in previously unimaginable and life-affirming ways.

Now, over two years on from those floods, my community is improved but far from restored. I, however, am restored, more than restored – I am transformed. I can turn back toward and step into my community once again. Now, as a counsellor, art therapist, friend and member of the community, I sit and walk alongside the grief and loss of others. Sometimes we talk, we drink tea, we cry, we paint or draw, we put voice to the experiences we survived, we weave strands of threads and threads of stories to create something new, we feel into and move the unutterable through our bodies, we speak unspeakable fears that have sat within us these past years and have grown heavy with shame, and we begin to lean toward new ways of being in which freedom and contentment and joy are possible. We support ourselves: *Have courage, dear hearts.* We ask: *What do you need?* And we listen for the answers that come.

I Don't Dance Like I Used To —Annamaria Weldon

ABL

For a year, following my diagnosis of Parkinson's disease, I didn't write any poems. The memoir I was busy with was my excuse, but in truth it was easier to dwell in the past. I didn't want to 'go deep'. Non-fiction prose is safer than poetry, where my creative process is unpredictable, unbound, as it scans the unconscious.

When I broke my silence, feelings I'd suppressed surfaced in unintended ways. That first poem was deliberately located at Lake Clifton, my happy place and the inspiration for the book I wrote about the five years I spent walking the wetlands of Yalgorup when I was well and vigorous. It was to be a nature poem. Then they appeared: shadows dressed as metaphors, but unmistakable as the emotions I hadn't owned up to. Including why I'd returned to poetry:

> When I talk words escape me, but poems
> catch them like birds in a mist-net.

It seems I was fed up with the relentless daily discipline required to meet the demands of a degenerative condition.

> The lake, vast and old, asks nothing of me.
> I count jetty boards to steady my gait.

What a relief that the lake takes me as I am: slower to breathe, to speak, to walk. It has no expectations. Often I've been told 'Please speak up, I can't hear you' in response to my weakened voice. 'Lift those knees higher!' my physiotherapist shouts during PD Warrior training. The alarm clock shatters every dawn, demanding I take time-sensitive medication. Check-out operators expect impossible acts of deftness from me: I can no longer tidily pocket receipts, Flybuys and credit cards while I swiftly lift shopping bags into my trolley. And even when I'm only halfway over the street crossing, the red pedestrian traffic light begins to flash, ticking loudly.

Re-reading my poem, it was also clear I resented the cruel bluntness of diagnostic language:

> Shimmering water suggests kinder words
> for shaking.

I asked a learned friend to read my poem. He agreed with me, adding: 'I noticed … references in the concluding lines to self-estrangement, an almost daemonic, involuntary re-making of the self (PD's rewiring of the brain) and, in the last line, your fear that the disease is even undermining/re-wiring your moral self'.[1]

> this wetland, where I learned old ways to mind
> the fragile, applaud divergence. And since
> illness rewired my brain, my body, I
> must care for this frail stranger, though it seems
> harder now to be wise or kind.[2]

My feelings bared on the page, I could no longer deny the frustration I had camouflaged as brave acceptance. I was *this frail stranger* who feared that chronic pain and disabling fatigue would soon overwhelm her better angels, reason and compassion. I was becoming less patient, more reactive, intolerant of others' foibles: *harder now to be wise or kind.*

I had so many questions. How carefully I had avoided them.

I hadn't ever consciously thought *why me?*

Why *not* me? Over a hundred thousand Australians live with Parkinson's. I have never thought of good health as an entitlement, because for decades I had severe migraines and allergies. And in my late forties, I lost my husband to lung cancer. He was fifty-two. My new partner's wife also died too young, of ovarian cancer. In our apartment building, one resident (who lives alone) is legally blind. A couple cares for their gravely ill child, who has never walked, talked or been able to see.

So why the wistfulness and the tinge of resentment detected in my lines? It wasn't as though I had been told I was going to die of Parkinson's. It isn't terminal, but incurable and degenerative. You die with PD, not because of it. My aforementioned friend also noted my writing contained 'a muted cry of unconsoled loss', hearing it give an '(again muted) voice to the stirrings of anger.'[3]

Perhaps it was because, for years, I'd hidden the pain and tiredness of fibromyalgia with a happy face, and minimised the breathlessness of my bronchiectasis – both invisible conditions. So, when I developed Parkinson's, I automatically covered that up as well. I minimised, I masked, I made sure to manage my workload and limit my social activities so as not to expose my weakness. I didn't want to seem a sympathy-seeker. I didn't want to be sidelined. Yet when the few people I did confide in, early on, remarked I didn't *look ill*, or *shake enough* or have *a blank expression*, strangely this upset me; it was as though some truth about me was being rejected, or worse, that I was an imposter.

Having now grown more fluent in the language of chronic, invisible conditions, I know ambivalence and confusion are common. I see that framing illness as 'weakness' is ableism – a term I had to look up. So was my fear that I'd be weeded out, professionally and socially, for disclosing my conditions. I have also challenged my assumption that revealing them would be seen as a plea for sympathy. Is that really how I regard others confronted with mental or physical health issues? Was I now 'othering' myself?

I am a work in progress, linguistically and attitudinally. That work requires the courage to confront my own shadows and change the script.

*

My other work-in-progress, writing a memoir, also demands courage. Brené Brown believes the original definition (from the Latin word *cor*, meaning 'heart') is to use your whole heart to tell the story of who you are.[4] There are many times bravery is required to do so honestly: to take responsibility for patterns revealed in reliving my past.

However, that process has also helped me trace how Parkinson's disease developed, literally under my nose, surreptitiously over a long time. Once research had shown me the signs, I recognised them in my own story. These signs are insidious. My experience is that they evade recognition as Parkinson's precursors, even when over time, each one is brought to a doctor's attention and treated.

Some are subtle: handwriting that becomes smaller, difficulty sleeping, nightmares, constipation, voice changes, fatigue, depression, anxiety and apathy. Presented as isolated issues, in my case during a span of about seven years, it was easy for medical practitioners to overlook the bigger picture. These common complaints can be put down to temporary stress, ageing, concurrent medical conditions – even outcomes of an acute injury.

In addition to this, the sequence of symptoms' appearance is different for everyone and the totality of symptoms varies from patient to patient. Not everyone has all of the symptoms simultaneously, or at all, certainly not initially. It often takes a few years to pinpoint Parkinson's as the underlying cause, even when, as I had, a patient presents with a persistent resting tremor in one hand and has had several falls, together with other motor symptoms such as walking more slowly and experiencing muscle stiffness – with or without pain. I had all these. But Parkinson's isn't solely a motor disorder.

Dopamine, the lack of which causes this condition, 'acts on areas of the brain to give you feelings of pleasure, satisfaction and motivation ... When you feel good, for example, when you achieve something or do something fun, it's because you have an increase of dopamine in the brain'.[5] Without dopamine, I gradually lost my enthusiasm for the very things that typified my personality. By the time I was diagnosed, I would stare in amazement at my female doctor's stylish necklace and wonder where she found the energy to bother. My dismay at this apathy (although I didn't call it that at the time; I thought I was lazy, ageing disgracefully and 'letting myself go') was compounded by the half-finished books lying about my home. I used to be a book reviewer. In that former life, I used to read three books a week!

Apathy, a direct effect of dopamine depletion, is a scourge that can rob a person of their self-respect. For years I mistook it for burnout, for depression, for tiredness. I reduced my workload, increased my antidepressants, took frequent naps. And it still remained beyond me to finish reading a book. Getting ready for any occasion that required attention to my dress and accessories was now a chore, instead of the joy it had always been. As a consequence, I felt ashamed. I felt guilty. I felt as though the lights were dimming in my brain.

When I was prescribed Madopar as the medication for my Parkinson's, it was like a renaissance. Astonished by the return of my concentration and enthusiasm, I kept a journal note of books I was devouring: from 20 June to Christmas 2022 I read twenty-four sizeable books of poetry, fiction and non-fiction. I've been told this is known as 'the honeymoon period'. Over time, some will find that the efficacy of medication wanes. I prefer to remind myself that Michael J. Fox, perhaps the most well-known PD patient, is still feeling its benefits after nineteen years.

The death of one's dopamine-producing brain cells, which causes Parkinson's (why these cells die, leaving patients with a mere twenty percent by the time of diagnosis, is another mystery) affects motivation, concentration, mood and memory, perception of smell and taste, the body's ability to regulate temperature and a host of mostly invisible, unpleasant but fugitive sensations. However, Parkinson's most recognised manifestations are physical. Which is why I don't dance like I used to. In fact, although I didn't know it at the time, that was my first clue.

*

It was the spring of 2013 in Western Australia. At Clancy's, Fremantle's famous fish and music venue, I was sixty-three, single and unaccustomed to going on dates, but life was lifting me out of my usual writer's rut: the book I'd been working on since 2009 had been accepted for publication and in two days I was flying to New South Wales on my own to attend the Watermark Literary Society's biennial muster. So when a new acquaintance invited me out for a drink and a dance, I accepted.

Lucky Oceans was in full swing onstage, patrons were thronging the dance floor and for the first time in years, I joined them. Jiving was as natural to me as swimming or trekking through bushland and despite my lack of practice, as a child of the 60s the moves were still there in my muscle memory. My friend was a musician who had a great sense of rhythm. Dancing with him was a delight. Until he spun me round and I almost lost my footing. Quickly covering it up, I concentrated fiercely on keeping my balance. I hadn't touched any alcohol so there was no explanation for my embarrassing lack of steadiness. Eventually I pleaded tiredness. We returned to our seats and my sugar-free Coke.

Fast-forward to 2019, by which time I had sold my house because I could no longer cope with a large place. Some of my symptoms were really worrying me. I had had four falls, a frozen shoulder. My hand tremor was a nuisance. Finally, my GP and I joined the dots. I waited three months for my initial neurology appointment at the Perron Institute for Neurological and Translational Science. Three years and two brain MRI scans later (to rule out other conditions) I had final confirmation of the PD diagnosis. The timing was challenging. With two books recently published, I was now midway through writing a memoir. In addition, my partner, Dennis, and I had booked to go on a month-long European trip in September 2023.

I threw myself into improving my fitness: to counter the typical paucity of movement that characterises Parkinson's, I attended classes with a physio three times a week, including PD Warrior sessions and occasional yin yoga. I joined Parkinson's WA. I invested in self-administered infrared light therapy. Working with a speech therapist helped me to give poetry recitals again.

Even so, re-reading my poem I realised how this condition had stirred up conflicting feelings: resentment at loss but also gratitude it wasn't worse; greater empathy and yet a tendency towards impatience. As a counsellor once told me, 'We are complex beings who can hold opposing emotions in balance.'

I repeated that wise observation recently, when I told a close friend of my frustration at comments like *at least you still have your mind* ... and *thank goodness you can still drive* ... And yet, I told her, I'm the first one to say those things too. Smiling, she reminded me of the Tim Minchin song 'Taboo (Ginger Song)', in which only a red-headed person can call another 'ginger'. She understood! Reassured, I confided that I was afraid of my forthcoming trip – the first since my Parkinson's diagnosis – of a month in Europe.

After a long flight from Perth, I was to travel with Dennis from the foot of Italy to the port of Amsterdam by coach, rail and ship. Because it's my nature and because I was fearful, I prepared carefully. I took advice from others who have travelled with Parkinson's, ensuring I had all my medications, a walking stick and excellent support during my trip.

And yet, such extended travel abroad felt risky. At home, I'd grown used to myriad lifestyle adaptations, to slowing down, to attending to the discipline of daily therapies. A busy travel itinerary would provide none of these. I remembered too well that, on three previous trips, I'd found steps, steep hills and crowded train stations a nightmare. How, undiagnosed for years, I'd tried to keep up with Dennis, assuming I was being a bit of a hypochondriac or a princess. I was used to apologising as I lagged behind his athletic stride and collapsed, exhausted, at the end of each day's sightseeing. But as I talked about India, Ireland, Spain, Malta, Japan, I also felt again the intoxicating freedom of travel, of climbing or walking (however painfully) to strange and wonderful places: up hundreds of steep steps to the top of a samurai castle in Himeji, Japan; more steps to the top of Thoor Ballylee, Yeats's tower in Galway; across the sprawling terraces of Granada's Alhambra. I'm so grateful for that conversation. Today, with a glorious month of travel to new places behind me, I can share that what I was most afraid of risking has in fact turned out to be my greatest healer.

In what way was travel my healer? It seduced me with distractions that pushed me beyond my limits. I came to those self-imposed boundaries, at which we stop when we feel too much pain, too much exhaustion, too little hope of accomplishing what we set out to do … and mostly, I overcame them. Sometimes only just. Sometimes with hell to pay afterwards – exhaustion and pain. But they passed, and the memories remain. Memories are so much more than emotions remembered and thoughts revisited. Moments fully lived are granular, cellular and remain embodied. Even limited by Parkinson's, this mind and body of mine continues to be an archive. In the movements of muscles, the pulse of blood, I contain catalogues, libraries of stories, galleries of images.

Travel has also given me another, perhaps even greater healing: over the previous eighteen months, my seemingly interminable daily schedule of precisely timed medications and physical therapy had been at the forefront of my attention. During the four weeks I travelled on a tour – and therefore always in the company of others – I integrated both these vital ingredients of my life seamlessly and discreetly into the day's activities. With a sense of unease, I realised how 'foregrounding' my condition while living at home had begun to define me.

Instead of something scheduled by the clock and undertaken with the supervision of physiotherapists, keeping active while travelling became a by-product of sightseeing. It was hard going at first, inevitably being the last in the walking group and juggling my cane, my backpack and my phone-camera, although Dennis was always by my side, helping. But as my fitness improved, what had seemed tests of endurance transformed into acts of exhilaration. Each village toured, every castle, cathedral, chairlift and vaporetto ride was a conquest! Previously, taking my medications had divided up my days, in much the same way that church bells once punctuated the lives of villagers. On tour, those intervals at which I regularly took my medicine were reduced to a mild buzzing on my wrist, as my Fitbit prompted me to reach for my water bottle and pillbox. I would swallow the meds without another thought, on the way to some marvellous piazza or driving through a forest or gliding by castles on the Rhine.

I returned home with a very altered perception of these routines. I carry them lightly now. While I still respected the importance of medicine and physical exercise, they have become as much a part of my life as brushing my teeth and making a meal. Most incurable conditions require commitment to therapy; without it, deterioration accelerates. As Michael J. Fox says, 'Parkinson's is the gift that keeps on taking.'[6] Like him, I am not letting it take away my expectations of living as fully as possible, even with the incremental losses this disease promises are in store for me.

Mobility, pain management and cognition are the minimum aspirations for quality of life. I want more, but it takes courage to reach for it. Not the fantasy variety, but everyday courage: getting out of bed, taking the first step towards a plan. I've got a renewed taste for travel and we are off again soon: I'll be whizzing through airports pushed on a wheelchair, borrowing one to visit museums, and sometimes sitting out entire tour days to rest and recuperate. I can't choose the low-budget travel options anymore: my days of walking up five flights of stairs to an inner-city Airbnb (or samurai temple) are in the past. From now on I'm defining my life not by what I can't do but by what I can.

She Doesn't Seem Autistic—Esther Ottaway

ABL, SH

I was a bright girl. I talked early and could read at age two. By five I was reading *National Geographic* and *Reader's Digest* and discussing the facts I learned with my parents and my schoolteacher grandmother. It seemed clear to them that I would be exceptional. But as I grew, mystifying gaps appeared in my development: I couldn't catch a ball, ride a bike or execute the actions of sports; I could barely eat, and was so underweight that schoolkids called me anorexic; I was wide-awake at night, but slept so heavily in the day that I could hardly stay awake; I would sit and stare at my homework until midnight, unable to start, lost in an agony of anxiety; if I tried to cook or do chores, I would burn and break things; I couldn't find my way around; and I was afraid of, and stressed by, just about everything. At school, I was terrified that my work would be less than perfect, and devastated by my peers' comments, which I couldn't socially interpret. Wanting to be a 'good girl', I would hold myself together under the pressures of school, then dissolve into hysterical sobbing when I reached home. Convinced that I must be being bullied or abused, my mother went to the teachers to investigate, who reported that they saw a polite, intelligent, well-behaved model student. I was something generation X had no name for: an autistic girl.

It is not known what the true prevalence of autism is in women, because studies were done on boys, and diagnostic criteria came from those studies. This is typical of what researcher Caroline Criado Perez terms the 'gender data gap'.[1] Girls and women with autism find it as disabling as men do, likely more so, since social expectations of girls and women are much higher; but women are usually without diagnosis, let alone assistance. They present differently to men, though not that differently: much of the problem with getting women diagnosed lies in a gender stereotype that says that they can't be autistic.

As well as its social, mental and emotional impacts, autistic women and children are sick with physical conditions. It's not well known, but almost all autistic people have chronic health conditions, such as connective tissue disorders (causing pain), hypotonia and dyspraxia (causing severe weakness and inability to execute the movements involved in daily tasks), eating disorders and gastrointestinal disorders (causing malnourishment), severe sleep disorders, and ear, nose and throat disorders. Nearly half of us, including me, are dealing with six physical conditions or more. But for women, of whom much is expected socially – usually, to be bright and bubbly – showing the traits of autism and chronic illness or disability is so shameful that we learn early to hide them.

My generation was taught, both implicitly and explicitly, to see disability as failure, illness as weakness. People from generation X are described as self-sufficient, results-oriented and hardworking. Australian culture is not one where you talk about disability or get listened to if you do. And autism in women was not even a concept as kids from gen X grew up in the 70s and 80s, research on girls lagging a full hundred years behind that done on boys, as is common in all fields of medicine. As a young woman, if I said I was 'tired' – the only term I had for the intense difficulty of fighting the crippling, nauseating need for daytime sleep that I would later learn was narcolepsy – I was lectured to 'go to bed earlier'. If I said I was 'anxious' – the only term I had for crushing episodes of dysphoria which put me in bed in the foetal position, crying – I was told that 'everyone gets a bit nervous'. If I said I was in physical pain all the time, or that I couldn't run the school-mandated five kilometres, I wasn't believed by gym teachers or doctors. If I told peers about any of these things, the conversation fell into an awkward silence. I learned that there was absolutely no recognition of, or sympathy for, my disabilities. I learned to stay quiet, and I learned to harden up.

I learned too well. By age fifteen, I could see my exceptional grades starting to slip, my memory impairments and pathological demand avoidance (inability to start or finish work) becoming more problematic. With the immature reasoning of a fifteen-year-old, I decided that I would ignore every physical and mental symptom of my disabilities, throw myself into full-time work and go to a gym three times a week. I would be strong. I would overcome, as the prevailing narrative of the era directed, and I would pretend I was as well and happy as the world dictated that a bright young woman should be. I later wrote about this time in a poem:

> By the nineties, real women
> wore power suits, did step aerobics
> and made up their minds to get over cancer.
> Running boardrooms, they ran away from me.[2]

I lasted four years, the last three months of which popping, every four hours, Codral, the now-regulated pseudoephedrine tablets, to mask my failing body's dripping nose, sore throat, headache, and body pain, and to enable me, as the Codral advertisements put it in their barely hidden 'harden up' message, to *soldier on*. When I look back on this time, the courage I showed both astounds me and makes me deeply uncomfortable. At nineteen, I had a breakdown, left work, and was diagnosed with chronic fatigue syndrome, the only label of the era that came even remotely close to describing my disabilities. And I knew, beyond any doubt, that I was a massive failure.

*

Twelve years later, I had my only child, and at seven she was diagnosed with ADHD. Finding that this qualified her for no support whatsoever at school and seeing her inability to function well at school, I began to homeschool her. My daughter made three good friends in the homeschool community, and over time, I became best friends with their mothers. We talked together regularly about the clear intelligence and talents of our daughters, but also their inexplicable problems and dysregulations: they couldn't sleep, they were exhausted all day, they hair-pulled due to severe anxiety, they had obsessive routines and sensory needs, they complained of constant pain, they were allergic to everything, they talked extensively about their particular interests but couldn't respond to a typical conversational flow, and they had devastating 'meltdowns' when the stress got too much.

We were exhausted, too, and with all of this going on, we walked on eggshells, trying to predict and prevent the triggers that would set our girls off. None of us knew about female autism. My daughter's otherwise excellent paediatrician never mentioned it to me. Slowly, and largely with the advent of social media, we began to piece together the puzzle, so that by the time my daughter was fifteen, I presented my conclusions to our paediatrician. My daughter received her diagnosis. And I knew I had also found mine.

*

I'm a poet, and I've observed over the years that I often write poems about personal truths long before those truths float up into my conscious awareness. Before I realised I had autism, as I was preparing a book for publication, I noticed there were six or seven poems about my difficulties and chronic illnesses, and I pulled them out of the book and set them aside, thinking they might turn into a small collection.

After the concept of my autism had occurred to me, I searched on Amazon for books about women and girls with autism, and was shocked to find only about twenty – in the world. Here was the data gap identified by Caroline Criado Perez, and here was the reason I, my daughter, and countless other women and girls were confounded and struggling alone: we were not represented in literature at all. Why did we, the untrained, time-poor, exhausted parents of distressed little girls, have to be the ones to research information paths that led us to autism – slowly and inefficiently, because we didn't know what we were looking for? Why did we have to educate ourselves in unfamiliar, medical language, translate our girls' symptoms into that language, bring the diagnosis to our doctors and specialists ourselves, and in the process wait years –in my daughter's case, almost a decade – for help? Because autistic people were expected, by the medical profession and by society, to be boys and men. By 2021, the idea had coalesced: I wanted to write a book, not only about my own experiences, but about women and girls with autism.

The poems flowed. Autism is a complex, multifaceted experience, and I found poetry, with its ability to carry a complex experience in a few words, and its flexibility of form, the perfect medium. One of the first poems puts the reader into the experience of sensory processing disorder:

Small talk [excerpt]

Hey it's great to visit you ow that light the weird smell of your dinner how have you been birds chirping a bus a barking dog a screaming neighbourhood child the kettle boiling someone closing a door what's been happening with you the prickly texture of the couch the washing-machine running the bitter taste of your brand of tea the temperature normal for you that burns my mouth the washing-machine deafening and vibrating into pain and here's Beverley O'Connor with another ABC news update oh do I look as though I'm miles away sorry [3]

Here were the words for my long-repressed childhood disabilities, and their social shame:

Candles Unattended: a clinical history [excerpt]
Dyspraxia, hypotonia

Dyspraxia was called Clumsy Child Syndrome until 1989.

clumsy children are less well-liked
and have low self-esteem

clumsy with its barrowload of slurs. My given names:
unco, *weakling*, *gawky*,
hurry-up, *useless*. Fruitlessly I practised
dancing and shooting hoops – picked only once

for netball, where I shut down, stock-still, bewildered.
Ten years of practice to master makeup, so never pretty.

fatigue is common, so much extra energy is expended
trying to execute physical movements

the concentration
of just walking of swallowing
turning the key in the lock
aiming the hair dryer so as not to incinerate
my hair, my family-joke name Candles Unattended
will I drop the baby, burn it in the bath?[4]

And words for the gendered ways in which being an autistic woman often means social death, more so than for an autistic man:

Can't Keep House Woman
Sensory distress, dyspraxia, pathological demand avoidance, ADHD

Can't Keep House Woman
can't have friends over
they step over half-empty plates and glasses
unfolded washing and animal litter
filthy pig sty how can anyone live like that
Can't Keep House Woman says
sorry sorry sorry
her shame aflame

Can't Keep House Man
has all his friends over
they step over half-empty plates and stubbies
dust and power cords
it's a bachelor pad!
They play Playstation
eat from pizza boxes laugh
slap him on the back
thanks for a great night, mate[5]

Writing the poems in *She Doesn't Seem Autistic* was both a painful re-examination and a loving reclamation of my history. I could see, for the first time, that I had not been a failure: I had been an undiagnosed and unsupported disabled child and young adult. What's more, I had been an incredibly strong and courageous child, young woman, and adult: I not only got through daily life but managed to excel academically; I carved out a successful, though very part-time, career as a writer in corporate communications and in the arts as a poet; and I coped with the overwhelming demands of raising a child who had significant complex needs.

Caroline Criado Perez's book is titled *Invisible Women*. As I wrote *She Doesn't Seem Autistic*, I found myself burning with rage at my experience of being rendered completely invisible as an autistic girl and woman. This poem of mine is now travelling on social media, and is something of an anthem:

There's no disabled girls with style like mine

A woman wearing makeup must be fine.
They tell me there is nothing wrong with you.
Disabled girls cannot have style like mine.

Good-looking girls are not supposed to whine
or carry on about what they can't do.
A woman wearing makeup must be fine

and healthy, strong, except when her waistline
is big: then the first thing she needs to do
is lose that weight. No girls with style like mine

have hidden disabilities, or climb
up mountains of distress. From birth, we knew
that little girls in dresses must be fine

and happy. When I talk about decline,
my sobbing, shattered meltdowns, self-harm, blue
nights, they fail to see, through style like mine,

my terrors, my self-medicating wine.
I dress well and it helps my grip stay true
on mental health. My fault for looking fine.

You're clearly well, don't waste the doctor's time.
Autistics do not look the way you do.
A woman wearing makeup must be fine.
There's no disabled girls with style like mine.[6]

But as I wrote the poems, some of them fiery, I was acutely aware that releasing this book would mean publicly identifying myself as autistic. Was I prepared to own this work? How much of my own experience did I really want to reveal to friends, relatives and employers? How could I be honest enough to make the poetry emotionally true and moving, yet navigate and buffer the degree to which it was personally exposing?

I knew I didn't have to release this book. I could stay silent. But my thoughts kept returning to those few books on Amazon, many of them purely medical, hardly any that offered emotional validation and support. I knew I could do that in my poems. And I thought about myself and my friends, how incredibly alone we had been in parenting our girls, with no-one seeing our struggles, no guideposts or help. I thought: someone has to step forward.

And I was buoyed by the support I received: my publisher, when I presented the idea of the book, immediately said they'd publish it; two arts funding bodies had given small grants to help support me while I wrote it; and my requests for book endorsements were all met warmly. Dr Michelle Garnett, one of the two leading clinical psychologists on female autism in Australia, replied to my request for a cover endorsement in an email: 'A big yes!'[7]

Occupational therapist and fellow poet Susan Austin was clear-eyed about the evident risks, but she also said she found it clever, brave and beautiful, and reminded me that at the end of the day, one wants 'to work for employers who judge you on your actual work and contribution and not your deficits or challenges, as any truly good employer would.'[8]

I decided I wanted to release the book. At forty-seven, I was so tired of disguising my experiences. I didn't know what the repercussions would be, but I felt they couldn't possibly result in situations harder than my life had been to this point. And where were the role models? I had to be one.

*

Expecting a tiny article of a few column inches about my upcoming launch of *She Doesn't Seem Autistic*, I opened my local paper. Instead, I found a double-page spread, with the headline POET BRAVELY LIFTS THE LID ON LIFE WITH AUTISM, and a large photo of my face.[9] Cold adrenaline flooded my stomach. I had done it now, for better or worse, and who knew what the outcomes might be?

Later that week, I stood in a room full of natural light and beautifully arranged native flowers, before a crowd of women and girls, from seven-year-olds through to women in their seventies. Friends were by my side as I spoke about my hidden disabilities and those of countless girls and women. Afterwards, as I signed books, the women came to me, one by one, saying that they had just found out they were autistic, or that their granddaughter was autistic, or that they were women practitioners supporting autistic girls. Every one of them thanked me. Every one received me with love and understanding. Every one bestowed the message: we see this side of you, and we respect you. Your work helps us. And I began to heal.

There is much work to do in encouraging the medical profession and society to look for autism in girls and women. Please, allow a bright, autistic girl to exist, in your mind, and in society around you. See these girls. Advocate for these girls, in whatever way you can.

Now, there are twenty-one books.

A Coin from the Man in the Moon – Natalie Damjanovich-Napoleon

MCS, PRG

I used to think courage was something people needed to climb Mount Everest, or to charge over a trench and face the enemy, or to fly to the moon in a rocketship. But my gruelling journey into pregnancy made me realise courage is something ordinary women and people with wombs have to find every day to face a world that does not listen to our bodies – or what we say is happening to them – with doctors and medical science dismissing our symptoms and ignoring our pain in equal measure.

*

'You're so brave!' my friend Donna insisted as I was about to embark on an around-the-world trip to meet someone I may or may not have been in love with.

I'm not brave, I thought as I trundled my suitcase and guitar to the Qantas check-in desk. *I'm not brave, I'm stupid*. But it was too late. With ticket in hand, at thirty-four, I was about to get on a plane to meet my friend Brett in Santa Barbara, California. Brett and I had been corresponding for two years, first via email and then with weekly phone calls, and slowly, maybe, falling in love. He had invited me to visit him after I told him I was doing an *Eat Pray Love*. That is, after my failure to get pregnant and my subsequent divorce, I was going on a worldwide trip in the hopes of finding myself.

*

Brett and I met when I was married to my first husband. Brett had written a glowing review of an EP we had recorded called *Fear of Falling*, referencing all our seminal influences: The Jayhawks, Gillian Welch, and Uncle Tupelo – all alt-country bands that only a handful of people in Australia knew about at the time. Our mutual friend Jasmine, from the band Halogen, had hooked us up, so next time Brett visited Perth to hang out with Jasmine, we met up for a drink. The three of us got along swimmingly. After that we'd call Brett every six months or so to discuss the latest music releases we'd been listening to – this was pre-internet, in the time of CDs, when people shared favourite music by word of mouth.

In 2003, when my marriage was disintegrating, in a last-ditch attempt to fix the twisted knot of our music careers and relationship, we decided to go to the United States and play some gigs and to explore the Americana music we loved. Brett had moved to Santa Barbara, so we decided to pay him a visit and play a few shows. He picked us up in Los Angeles and drove us to Santa Barbara, taking us the scenic way along Highway 1 on the Pacific Coast Highway. I was entranced, staring at the Pacific in wonder, noticing how different the colour of the ocean was in California from back home: a choppy deep blue-green that both swallowed me up and welcomed me in.

The three days we spent in Santa Barbara were uneventful: we played a gig to about twenty people in a bar that is now long gone, and went sightseeing, ate great American breakfasts, and I fell in love with hash browns and endless cups of steaming-hot drip coffee. The most telling memento I have from that trip is a photo of Brett and me standing at the train station in Santa Barbara, his arm around my shoulder, looking as if we were a couple already. No intimate words nor touch had passed between us, yet that photo contained a premonition of my future life.

*

Three years after my solo around-the-world trip, at thirty-seven, the same thought that was in my head as I boarded the plane to see Brett again entered my mind as I lay in a hospital bed – *This is not brave, it's stupid*. Brett was holding my hand while I was hopped up on pre-op meds about to have exploratory surgery that would hopefully provide an answer to my infertility issues. I had spent five years of my life trying to get pregnant, enduring a myriad of treatments – conventional to kooky – the flaming plane crash to earth ending of my first marriage, and the near Stockholm syndrome breakdown of my sense of self in the process. How could I trust anything that my body was telling me, that *something was not right*, when I had been told so many times that I was wrong?

This is not brave, it's stupid, I thought as I waited to be wheeled into the operating theatre. Inside I was quivering with fear. Brett knew my story, how my ex had cheated on me while I was stabbing myself with fertility drugs, and how scared I was of surgery. My fear was compounded by my distrust of doctors since my symptoms had been dismissed so many times in the past.

'Here,' Brett said, 'take this.'

Lying on a gurney I was feeling dopey and confused from the pre-op meds. He placed a silver coin into my hand.

'You want me to buy something from the vending machine?'

'No,' he said. 'This is a special coin I got for you – it's for good luck.'

'Good luck?' I questioned in a whisper as I held up the coin to examine it.

'Yes, good luck,' he said. 'It's a coin from NASA that contains metal flown to the moon and back during the Apollo missions.'

Brett knew I collected coins, especially rare and interesting ones. I was so overwhelmed I could barely croak out a 'Thank you, darling.'

'You're as brave as those astronauts that went to the moon,' he whispered. 'You've got this.'

I looked at him, blinking back the tears that were welling in my eyes.

I'd been through so much already; I was afraid I could not survive another failed attempt at a solution to my infertility problems. This shiny, fat coin gave me hope. If women and men could have the courage to get into a rocket, or a space shuttle full of fuel that could explode on the launchpad or disintegrate when escaping the earth's atmosphere, then I could have surgery to find the answers I had been looking for.

*

The first time I went to a doctor specifically to discuss problems with my period, I was in my early twenties. I told him that something 'didn't feel right' and that my periods were heavy and painful each month. He asked if I was depressed, and I said yes, at times having painful periods made me feel down. He offered me antidepressants. I refused his offer knowing that depression was not my main problem, my period was.

Later, at the same surgery, I saw another doctor, once again expressing my concerns at my period being heavy – there were times when I passed chunks that looked like pieces of liver, I always bled through my pads at night and the stabbing pains when I got my period were often unbearable. On this occasion a doctor had the audacity to draw me a diagram to show me how a period works, pointing out that 'you only lose eight tablespoons of blood' during 'menstruation'. No blood tests or internal examinations were made, and I was sent on my way empty-handed, except for a diagram on a piece of paper. I felt like I had been metaphorically patted on the head like a child, and now that I had been lectured on how my body worked, the pain and symptoms I was experiencing were expected to magically go away. They did not.

The third time I saw a doctor at the same surgery, I was sure this time I would get it right. I would go to a female doctor; I would tell her I had a university degree, so she knew I was intelligent. Surely, she wouldn't draw anatomical diagrams, treating me like I was uninformed, because she had a uterus too. I was wrong. I gave her the same list of symptoms, the same story. And received the same blank look, and little acknowledgement of my symptoms. She gave me a script for the contraceptive pill. Once on the pill some of my symptoms subsided, so I gaslighted myself into believing I had been imagining how bad the signs had been all along.

The conclusion I came to was that I was obviously wrong about my own body – the period pain, the heavy periods, the massive mood swings, the two times I had fainted when I had my period and the gastric upset on my first few days were all 'normal'. I mean, how could I be right about what I was experiencing in my own body when three doctors had told me I was mistaken? In these doctors' eyes, I was either depressed, daft or overreacting. Although a part of me didn't believe them, I was done with telling my story and being ignored. So I buried what they said deep inside, tolerating what was handed to me, like women before me had done for centuries.

It was as if, in my silence about my pain, I carried the stories of all the women who had come before me. Like a 'hysterical' Victorian woman with postnatal depression locked in an attic driven mad by yellow wallpaper, or a woman in the Middle Ages in Scotland who cried for pain relief during birth and was burned at the stake for her complaints, I knew I had to shut up about my pain or suffer the consequences.

It wasn't until a decade later that I revealed to another doctor the issues I had with my period. My first marriage was in its final throes, and I had finally found a gynaecologist who would listen to me, after three years of trying to get pregnant naturally, trying a raft of different approaches with no success. She wanted to do exploratory surgery to find out what was causing my infertility issues; 'endometriosis' was never mentioned. Months later my marriage fell apart, so I cancelled the surgery.

The second time I told a doctor about my period I was ready and with the right person, Brett. Sitting in a fertility doctor's office in Santa Barbara, he asked me questions no doctor had ever asked before.

*

'How long have you been trying to fall pregnant?'

'In total, about five years.'

'Do you experience painful periods?'

'Kind of, they're not too bad.' I downplayed the pain because I had already been labelled a 'faker.' Having lived with that label for ten years, I didn't want it on my medical file again.

'Do you experience pain during sex?'

'No, well … sometimes, yeah, maybe. Does this even matter?' I toned down the pain during sex because, again, who wants to be labelled by a fourth doctor as 'overreacting'?

'I don't think you have endometriosis. But since the dye test showed that you have a kink in your right fallopian tube, I think we should at least go in, straighten out your fallopian tube, or remove it if we must, and then do a D and C procedure while we're there.'

'I really appreciate that you're looking into this.'

'Talk to the receptionist on the way out and she'll schedule your surgery.'

'Thank you. Thanks again. Thank you so much.' I gushed because I had been dismissed for so long by doctors that anyone who listened to me was, to my mind, like a god in human form.

*

The World Health Organization defines endometriosis as 'a disease in which tissue similar to the lining of the uterus grows outside the uterus. It can cause severe pain in the pelvis and make it harder to get pregnant'.[1] It is the leading cause of pelvic pain and infertility and is estimated to affect around 176 million women worldwide.[2]

The symptoms of endometriosis, or 'endo' for its sufferers, are painful periods, heavy periods, irregular periods, pain during bowel movements or urination, painful sex, bloating, anxiety, depression, and trouble getting pregnant, among others. I often wonder if the symptoms of 'anxiety' and 'depression' are due to the fact that, on average, most endo sufferers have to wait a decade to be diagnosed with the condition and, therefore, to be believed and treated accordingly. Although, with rising awareness about the disease, diagnosis has been recently cut down to seven years.

In her memoir about her experience with endometriosis, *Pain and Prejudice*, Gabrielle Jackson writes about how in medical situations women's physical suffering is often incorrectly diagnosed or disregarded because medicine has predominantly used men as the default human body, leaving women's pain as mostly misunderstood and perceived as being deviant or uncommon.[3]

My story is typical and similar to many people's journeys with endometriosis. For almost two decades I had suffered in silence; doctors had ignored me and patronised me, effectively treating me as a 'hysterical' female. In the process they had destroyed my trust in my own body and – up to this point – my faith in the medical profession.

*

The simple day surgery I went in for in Santa Barbara ended up being a five-hour procedure. The doctor found five lesions of endometriosis in my abdominal cavity, which he burned out, and a 'chocolate cyst' on one ovary, an endometrial blood-filled cyst, which he burst. He gave me a D and C and pushed more dye through my fallopian tube to straighten it out. My condition was recorded as 'moderate' endometriosis.

Almost seventeen years since I first went to a doctor with my symptoms, I finally had an answer to the pain and suffering I had been through since my twenties and the infertility I had dealt with since I was thirty. I had endometriosis.

*

Two months after having surgery I took the drug Clomid, which stimulates ovulation, and fell pregnant at the age of thirty-seven for the first time in my life. I was not afraid. The day I found out I was pregnant I felt like I was walking on clouds, and, apart from my wedding day with Brett, I cannot recall a more momentous day in my life. Later, after reading a medical paper, I discovered there is a magical three- to six- month window endometriosis patients have after having endo lesions removed to fall pregnant: after that, their chances of becoming pregnant are reduced by this insidious disease once again. This indicates how fast endometrial cells regrow, even after surgery.

Nine and a half months after discovering I was pregnant, I gave birth to my son, Samuel, a healthy, strapping baby boy. I chose to try to give birth naturally with the assistance of midwives, without drugs or medical intervention, unless necessary, because I wanted to be in control. I wanted to trust my own body. My body triumphantly delivered.

I am grateful to the people who listened to me: my husband, my fertility doctor in Santa Barbara, and especially other women who always knew I was telling the truth. However, my trust for medical practitioners remains tenuous, and it is still difficult for me have faith in doctors. I often have to see several doctors before I find one, who I can tell is listening, *actually* listening to me, instead of seeing me with their blinkered perceptions. I want to be heard as a person who knows their own body, not perceived to be the unreliable narrator of the story of my own health.

As Gabrielle Jackson points out, for the diagnosis and treatment of endometriosis to improve for women and gender-diverse individuals, the medical profession needs to end their sexist perceptions.[4] Claiming to have knowledge of the human body, yet not studying women's bodies or believing women's pain, has led to the breakdown of faith women have in medicine and doctors.[5] We can and need to do better.

Making change like this *isn't* brave, it's simply good medicine.

*

Since my diagnosis, I have joined several endometriosis support groups online. The stories of these women and gender-diverse people show true courage. In these groups, people tell stories of how they have been accused of being drug-seekers when they have sought relief for their debilitating pain; labelled as mentally ill, when they are not, in situations where they continue to tell doctors about their symptoms and seek answers; and countless stories of women sent away from the ED with endo flares, in extreme pain, when they have nowhere else to go, then being sent away with inadequate treatment or diagnosis. Every day these women have the courage to seek answers for a disease where there is no cure, and no diagnostic tool other than laparoscopy, an expensive and invasive surgery.

The moon coin sits in my bedside drawer, and I still pull it out every now and again and turn it over in my hands when I need some courage. The coin itself doesn't give me courage. It reminds me I have courage of my own that I have earned through living a life with a womb and stepping out into the world every day. It reminds me I have the courage of the collective, the endo warriors who walk this path with me.

As of the day I write this, twelve men and no women have been on the surface of the moon. The first female astronaut is projected to step on the moon through a NASA mission in late 2024.

The metal in the coin I was given has been to the moon and back; in many ways I feel the distance I have covered in my endometriosis journey – like the ongoing journey of female astronauts – has been just as vast.

The Fray—Jo Giles

DTH, MT

I watch the clock. I try to not to watch the clock but then, again, I watch the clock. Each glance, each tick of the second hand reminds me time is immutable. It will not slow for you. It will not wait for your breathing to improve, nor will it pause while you attempt to increase your food intake so you're not just a whisper of yourself struggling to function. That clock on the wall across from your hospital bed reminds you how far you need to travel to stay alive. The cystic fibrosis nurse practitioner, Sue, tells your doctors you always 'rally' and that you have what it takes to live. But you know, right now, in this moment, you are a splinter away from death. You vow to hold on.

I am moved from the respiratory ward to the intensive care unit. The ventilators – machines that manage your breathing for you when your abdominal muscles are so worn out they are failing at the task – are better in ICU, more effective. Breathing takes priority over eating as removing the mask for food starves my brain of oxygen. I'm panicking. I'm dying. My body is failing. My ICU nurse tells me they need to insert a nasogastric tube. This woeful procedure requires me to swallow a seemingly endless plastic tube, inserted into the nostril, past my throat, into my oesophagus and into my stomach.

She inserts the NG tube and I can feel the plastic against my throat. It is asphyxiating. My heart races, *bang bang*, against my chest. I can't breathe and my body violently rejects the tube. I'm choking, gagging. The tube is whipped out and she looks on quietly as I gasp for air. Tears are pouring out of my eyes and down my cheeks between the mask and my skin. I have so little air I can't spend it on anger and frustration, but I will. How am I supposed to stop my breath to swallow when I am always in the midst of breathing? This panting, gasping, starving-for-oxygen kind of breathing. They say end-stage lung disease is like running a marathon, all the time, every day. I thought they were exaggerating.

I was wrong.

We try to insert the tube twice more before we quit. It's late. I'm exhausted. Everyone has gone home; my sister, Chris, also, has gone. It's quiet and I'm alone in my dying. Then, through the quiet, I can see two people talking outside my room. It's my nurse and someone else, I think it could be Jamie, the cystic fibrosis physio. They move slightly and the nurse lifts her hand as if to comfort. I want to leap out of bed and tell him not to worry, that everything is fine. Tomorrow will be a better day and I'm not as sick as everyone thinks I am. I'll bounce back like I always do. You'll see, Jamie, you'll all see.

*

The ICU doctor thinks I'm in a hopeless situation. This hopeless woman with her hopeless lungs. Can't swallow the nasogastric tube. Can't breathe. Can't fight. Her carbon dioxide levels rising towards a state of narcosis. She'll become sleepy and confused. She'll drift away into a dreamless sleep and die – probably tonight. Her medical team can't accept reality. Won't listen to me. I'm only the doctor.

I imagine him rolling his eyes as if he's the only person in the room who understands what is happening. What will happen.

Now that I'm alone, he asks to speak with me. He calls me 'Miss Giles' at first. Then he slips into a more intimate 'Jo'. Like he knows me. Like we're in this together. I prefer the casual first-name basis approach. But I recognise the manipulation. He drags a chair over to my bed and leans in as if we are confidantes. He tells me it's his job to say the non-invasive ventilation isn't working as well as they would like.

'We need to intubate you,' he says, dropping this procedure into the conversation like it's our only option. No big thing. But it *is* big. They insert a tube down into your trachea to breathe for you. Like I'm having surgery. It requires a general anaesthetic, and my lungs are too weak. It would mean my death. It also means the lung transplant team at Fiona Stanley Hospital won't give me the transplant I need.

'You're dying, Jo,' he says. 'We've tried the NG tube three times now without success. You're too weak to tolerate the procedure. You need nutrients. Your organs are beginning to shut down. We can keep you alive till your family has a chance to say goodbye, but that's all we can do. I'm concerned your team isn't telling you this. There's no lung transplant.'

He pauses, waiting for me to say something, and I wonder what it is he expects me to say. I wonder how many times he's done this and whether all his patients have trusted him. Did they acquiesce? Or did they fight?

I was seventeen years old when I first sat with someone about to die. Not quite mature enough to understand my role but old enough to figure it out. I met Ray at a CF camp at Point Walter on the Swan River in Perth and afterwards, when I returned to Northam, we became avid penpals. Six months later, in the winter, he was dying. I had visited him a few times earlier in the year and noticed he was weaker than I remembered. He was tiny, his pale, almost translucent skin stretched over his bones. He moved carefully, conserving breath, trying to hide his discomfort from me. I was silly enough in my refusal to think about his death, not now, not when I was starting to love him. This little elf-like creature who seemed to adore me, half my size, chasing me around the campground to hug me with his little 'tennis-racquet' arms. He had enchanted me – so how could he die? When his mother, Edith, called me to urge me to come see him, I was thinking I'd walk in, and he'd sit up and recover. I was disabused of that fantasy as soon as I stepped across the doorway into his room. The lights were dimmed, the blinds were drawn, and even now, decades later, I can feel that sense of death: thick, oppressive, final. He was asleep, but even in sleep, his agony was apparent. It was like he knew I was there, but the curtain of life and death hung between us. I sat with him all weekend. Sometimes he would talk and other times he'd mumble through sleep, struggling to breathe through the morphine and oxygen mask. Upon my parents' insistence, I was called home. I kissed him on the forehead and told him I loved him and that I'd see him soon. He died Monday morning.

I keep my feelings tightly wound but I sense an unravelling. No transplant? What is all this holding on for if there's no transplant? What are we doing here, trapped in an ongoing and endless scream, if this is it? No last-ditch effort, no final sprint to the finish. He can't be right. This doctor, this peripheral character, doesn't know me. He hasn't seen me fight. I race through his words looking for a way out. A space through which I emerge and crush his death sentence.

Show him how wrong he is.

'Thank you for telling me,' I say. 'I understand.'

Then I turn away.

Part of you wants to run, to leap from this room filling with death. You can't stop it. You want to rush outside and be with living things, touch them, smell them. Be amongst the permanence of old eucalypts, gently swipe your finger along the soft petals of flowers, immerse yourself in life. At the same time, you want to stay, to be with the person who is dying, to never leave. You might even believe your presence keeps them here and that they won't die if you can just stay.

'Not yet,' you'll whisper. 'Not yet.'

At the end, you'll want to be with them when they die. To hold them, stroke their hair, kiss their face. You will want to remind them: You were loved. You were loved. You were loved.

My ICU nurse returns in the morning, and I ask if there is something we can do to facilitate the insertion of the NG tube. I try to sit up. To look interested in staying alive. She nods a little and looks over at the doctor as if reluctant to contradict his advice, but I am not looking at him and I barely notice when he leaves.

There are, apparently, three things we can do. Firstly: use a smaller tube. Secondly, apply a topical anaesthetic so the edges of the tube don't hurt you when they scrape against your throat. Thirdly, drink water as you swallow. Think of the tube as one giant pill.

There is a fourth, but it involves a little luck. Ask the person who teaches students how to insert NG tubes to insert yours.

We succeed, which means they can 'feed' me bags of milky, pink fluid and administer medication via a syringe, directly into my NG tube. I start to improve. It's slow at first, like my leaves are no longer wilting. During the day the ICU nurse tells me that Sue stood outside my room all night to prevent the ICU team from intubating me. All. Fucking. Night.

Months after my transplant I remember this moment. Sue was the only one who fully believed I could make it. She made me believe it. She fought for me when I couldn't fight for myself and she did it so seamlessly I very nearly failed to notice.

'You know, I'm rather fond of you,' I tell her.

'I'm rather fond of you too,' she says.

They move me back to the respiratory ward. I am still close to dying but Sue has more control here. Nobody will decide to put me on life support here. Nobody will tell me there's no transplant there. I have a plan. Don't give up. Distract your mind. The clock has moved five minutes. I make a pledge to commit to another five minutes. Then another. And another.

It hurts to move. I lie on one side for a while until it's no longer tolerable and then I turn over. The discomfort is never-ending. The pain is becoming intolerable. It's the feeling of not being able to breathe. Even with non-invasive ventilation and oxygen, it simply isn't enough. The strap on my mask has to be tight so the air doesn't escape from the rubber seal around my nose and mouth. It is always slipping. So we tighten the strap and the weight of it is heavy. I can't sit up without leaning forward but then my back aches. I lean against the mountain of pillows behind me but then the fluid in my chest presses against my lungs and I can't breathe. I lurch back and forth trying to find a place where it is comfortable but there is no comfort in dying. I want it to stop. In these moments I wonder what I'm doing. This trying to stay alive. Is it worth it? Am I worth it? Am I prolonging my suffering? Am I prolonging the suffering of everyone around me – my family and the people who work here who have known me for years. Are we all suffering because I refuse to let go? I just don't know.

*

A doctor from the lung transplant team comes to see me. My sister, Chris, is there. Jamie and Sue stand behind her. A couple of my nurses are close by. The doctor sits opposite them on the other side of my bed. He has come to discuss transplant eligibility and I can see the conflict in his face. The weight of this decision. It is a hard decision. Transplant recipients are, usually, not this sick. It becomes unsafe. A waste of lungs. I want to tell him it's okay to say no. He shouldn't have to bear this burden. He exhales and quietly mutters, 'I hate this part.' I realise he's going to say no. I'm too far gone. I should have fought harder.

Then he speaks in a voice that everyone can hear.

'If you can gain weight …' The rest of his answer is lost in the relief of its aftermath. It's a chance. A glimmer of a possibility. A lifeline. I grabbed it as if I'd been drowning for years.

Years later the doctor and I talk about this moment. He always thinks he said 'no' and I always think he said 'yes'. I know that transplanting me was a risk and that keeping me alive was tenuous. I know he, most likely, should've said no. We could've lost it all. It is no small thing.

It takes about six weeks before I'm transplant-ready. As soon as I hit fifty kilos I relax. Now they can list me. I am transplant eligible. A week or two after that, the transplant coordinator, Sharon, calls the ward. My night nurse, who brings me snacks and a lucky hairband and sits with me when I can't sleep, wakes me at 5 a.m. with a cup of tea.

'They have lungs, Jo,' she says. She is smiling.

It is a long and disruptive expedition from sleep to wakefulness when you're in end-stage lung disease, but I can almost grasp what she's saying. There's a pair of lungs for me. After all my staring at the clock and refusing to succumb to death, in these final moments before my transplant, I choke.

'I'm not ready.'

Then I start to cry.

Just after my sojourn in the ICU, my friend, Jane comes to see me. I am in the High Dependency Unit on the respiratory ward, G54. Jane also has cystic fibrosis and, in a few years or so, she will have her own lung transplant. She believes, that when she was a soul, she chose to have CF. She says we all choose. She sits in the chair next to my bed. I am a pitiful sight. I know that almost everyone – the nursing staff, the transplant team, the social worker – they all think I'll die.

'Jo,' Jane says. 'It's okay to let go.'

I close my eyes. I can feel the rage surge inside. How dare she say this to me. Who is she to tell me or even suggest it's time to give in? It's not just bad advice; I can forgive her believing it would be better to go peacefully than endure this struggle, to suffer like this. After all, I am on the edge. Cadaverous. Ghostly. It's the presumption, I suppose, that it is her place to say this to me. I roll myself in bed in a heavy, slow turn, my ventilator mask and its attached hose, the oxygen tube, the wires and cannulas attached to my body, to lock my eyes with hers. To show I'm serious.

'Jane,' I say, with some effort. 'I'm not remotely close to being ready to have this conversation.'

At times I find it funny that my first instinct, when told there were lungs for me, was to say no. I wonder what it is in me that steps back when I have fought so hard to arrive at somewhere I want or need to be. It's a little sad that something in me thinks that I never deserve a chance. It still happens, even though I know that everyone deserves a chance. Everyone is worth being saved. We are all clamouring to be where we want to be.

I am racing through white corridors, attached to machines that monitor heart rate, blood pressure and oxygen saturation, dressed in hospital white. I am connected to the apparatus of medicine. Porous, random, cyborg, spectre, phantom. Not alive but neither am I dead. I feel the weight of my determination to live, lift. I will no longer have to watch clocks and make deals to hold on. My struggle is done. Whatever the outcome, death or life, I am ready.

Breaking the Silence: The Courage to Speak and to Know Differently—Penny Jane Burke

AB, DV, SA

Personal experience is a powerful source of knowledge and knowing. When personal experience is recognised for its transformative potential, we sow the seeds for social change and gender equality. The personal is the political, and from this wise feminist insight we can break the silence of gender-based violence, a lethal social problem of epidemic proportions that has detrimental effects personally and societally.

Whenever I have had the honour of holding a public platform, I have dug deep to find the courage to utter seven disruptive words: 'I am a survivor of domestic violence.' Afterwards, I am often approached by a woman who tells me in a hushed voice, 'I haven't told anyone before but … I am also a survivor of domestic violence.' These exchanges remind me why it is so important to refuse to collude in the silencing of this massive social problem experienced by so many women. According to a 2021 report from the World Health Organization, up to 753 million women globally have experienced physical or sexual intimate partner violence from the age of fifteen.[1] In Australia, at least a quarter of women experience violence at the hands of their partner or former partner. The numbers are worse for women with disabilities, Aboriginal and Torres Strait Islander women, women from disadvantaged socioeconomic and/or rural and remote areas, and LGBTQIA+ communities.[2] On average, one Australian woman a week is killed by her partner or former partner.[3] The figures are staggering, even more so when contemplating the hidden experiences that the statistics can't capture.

Politically, violence against women is widely perceived as a 'special' concern, outside of mainstream social policy. Home is overwhelmingly represented as a place of comfort, refuge and solace, making it difficult to articulate experiences of domestic, family and sexual violence in the public realm. Yet home is regularly a place of violence, danger and surveillance, a fact that is largely unspeakable and unknowable in the mainstream imagination of 'home'.

*

I am a survivor of domestic violence. Over thirty-five years ago, I was a prisoner of the house with my baby, tortured, physically and sexually abused, held under relentless surveillance, sleep- and food-deprived and so petrified for my life that I can still smell the dreadful sweat of terror emanating from my body. I was not allowed to have my own money, my official documents were hidden from me, and I was not permitted to see a doctor or receive healthcare during my pregnancy and after the birth of my baby. I was alone. Isolated. Young, terrified and destabilised. Dislocated from my home town and overnight forcibly taken overseas, my dreams and aspirations of being a ballerina were exploited and then trampled on. Over time, the gaslighting and manipulation left me in a state of profound confusion and disorientation; I no longer could speak or know. I no longer knew who I was. I was silenced and felt erased, almost non-existent. Often believing I would be better off dead than alive, but also determined to live to protect my baby, I saw no escape and could not bear the lifetime of abuse and suffering that seemed inevitable. Yet a flame of self-determination ran deep within me. 'You can beat me, you can kill me, but you will never take my soul,' I shouted in a moment of bold resistance to my abuser. My husband. The father of my beloved child. A man I loved. Till death do we part. He said I was his forever and ever – beyond this world and into the next. There was no escape. I had a duty. He was mentally ill, and so I needed to stand by him as his wife, I told myself. 'You made your bed; you must lie in it', my grandmother's words, totally out of context, ran in my head. 'If you ever leave me, I will kill everyone you have ever loved,' he hissed in my ear. He continually demonstrated his power and control over me in ways that remain unspeakable. How could I ever find a way forward?

*

Insidious trauma is as impactful as physical and sexual violence. The fear of what could happen outweighs the knowledge of what is happening. Better to stay in the situation you know than to risk fleeing. This is reinforced by the evidence that tells us women are at greater risk of losing their lives during the period of escape. The emotional and psychological trauma woven into constant physical and sexual abuse does ongoing harm to the soul and to the spirit. Shame is a powerful weapon of coercive control privately and publicly. Shame is felt as a deeply intimate sensation that damages the life force: 'I am not good enough; I never will be good enough'. Misogyny is sustained through subtle – and not so subtle – shaming of those who do not comply with the dominant order. Shame silences. Shame conceals. Shame keeps secrets, closely held in the body to hide the violence that is so shameful for the victim it can be kept tightly behind the mask of courageous survival. Survivors are expected to demonstrate extraordinary levels of resilience in the face of the social epidemic of gender-based violence.

*

For three years of inexorable emotional, physical and sexual violence, the shame of my situation as an abused wife kept me silent. I was a ghost of myself physically and spiritually. Until one day all the horror stored inside erupted as an unexpected sliver of a window to potential freedom was opened. I was suddenly taken by my delusional husband to Heathrow Airport under his strict control, his fingernails digging sharply into my neck, my passport in his possession, our baby in my arms and his menacing whisper sharp as a knife in my ear: 'Penny will say nothing' (by this point he only spoke in the third person). Suddenly I gained sight of two tall policemen walking in our direction, and just as they passed us, I gathered every ounce of courage in my body and screamed out with all my might for their help. My husband quickly grabbed our baby son from my arms and ran off with him in the other direction. I desperately tried to explain the situation, my hair matted, dark circles under my eyes, my skin pasty and my body emaciated by malnourishment. After some confusion and reluctance to aid me, a more senior and experienced officer joined us and intervened, directing the junior officers to immediately locate my husband and baby. Once they did, the three of us were taken to the police station in separate vehicles, him to be questioned, baby and me to receive breakfast and support. Three years of misery and captivity exploded in words that would not stop, and I was given the assistance I urgently needed. With their advice, I immediately found my way to a women's aid refuge as an emergency client, where I spoke to anyone who would listen, and I spent every night, my little son finally peaceful in bed beside me, writing pages upon pages of the trauma I had endured. I didn't understand then that I was self-counselling through journalling, and this process significantly contributed to restabilising my life and wellbeing. But this could not be done alone.

A beautiful soul, another survivor who worked at the women's aid refuge, held my hand, kissed my cheeks, wiped my tears and showed me the way forward. This was no easy road: my son and I had to constantly be on the move to dodge the threat of being recaptured or even killed, so with her help we lived in temporary conditions in multiple refuges across the greater London region. We finally gained some stability through social housing a year later, again with her assistance. She helped me secure legal aid and an outstanding solicitor who had domestic violence expertise and provided specialist support over many years of traumatising court episodes. My friend literally was my navigator, opening my eyes, astutely hearing my stories and guiding me through the maze of public services until finally the door of higher education was opened to me.

*

Higher education certainly is not a perfect world, but it changed my life direction. I became impassioned with a sense of social responsibility. I asked myself: how could other survivors of domestic violence have access to the transformative world I discovered through university study? The voices of inspirational women writers who would not be silenced by the social shame of misogyny, racism and violence replenished my spirit. Simone de Beauvoir opened my eyes to the social becoming and subordination of woman as the second sex; Angela Davis showed me that sexism, classism and racism were thoroughly entwined to sustain relations of oppression; Patti Lather taught me that empowerment is complex because power is always fluid and dynamic. Knowledge-making became accessible in new and exciting ways, and I found a pathway to a Women's Studies and Education program through the suggestion of a friend who read my honours dissertation and encouraged me to undertake a postgraduate degree. His recognition that my research on women's access to higher education was important work totally shifted my self-perception.

Recognition felt so different to shame. New avenues were opened to me. Yet the shame of trauma was so insidious I could only walk a narrow path: the one where I believed I could make a difference to other women or to my children. But I still did not believe in my own self. I was continuously in a state of displacement, of unbelonging, of self-disorientation. When told that doing a PhD on the impact of domestic violence on women's access to higher education was not a legitimate agenda for doctoral research, I buried my aspirations for challenging gender-based violence through research deep inside of me. Instead, I followed the advice to broaden my focus and undertook doctoral studies on the experiences of students accessing higher education, enabled through a Research Council Scholarship – which, I was told, were like 'gold dust'. This spurred me on despite my self-doubt and I continued to research who is seen as having the right to higher education and on what terms. Through the language of feminist, decolonial and anti-racist theory and practice, and over many years of dedicated research, I developed an authorial voice of my own. I found the courage to speak and write about misrecognition and its impact on higher education access and participation. Misrecognition is the unequal cultural value order that sustains misogyny and produces social and gender injustice. It enables the denigration of personhoods already marginalised through histories of oppression and inequality. It manifests in a sense of personal shame, redirecting attention away from the unequal social relations that produce feelings of unworthiness, exclusion and isolation. This enables gender-based violence to be another hidden dimension of the social fabric of oppressive and unequal relations.

*

At the start of my educational and research journey, I remarried to a man who was gentle and supportive, and we created an instant family: his son, my son and then came our third son soon after. As our three sons grew, I studied and drew strength from the feminist insights and principles that guided me on the messy life projects of becoming a scholar and developing as a mother. As my career developed and I progressed to more senior academic positions, I learned that I could lead differently through these feminist insights and principles with inclusive effects. The approaches I discovered through my engagement with feminist insights profoundly shaped my practices in all aspects of my life, as a mother, researcher, teacher, leader and writer. Yet still I felt blocked from experiencing the full joy of my discoveries. I felt the joy of my achievements and life projects at moments, in a fragmented way, but I still carried the heaviness of shame in the pit of my stomach, a pain that flowed in my veins as a form of not belonging, unworthiness and fear.

Insidious trauma runs deep. It is embodied. It is corrosive. It limits a sense of personhood and the capacity to take up space. I apologised for myself a lot. My grandfather, a loving, inspiring and enabling person in my life, suggested that I needed to stop saying sorry as it undermined me. My partner told me that I was a powerful woman with the capacity to make a difference in the world. My sons reminded me that I had transformed our lives and that I was a survivor because I was the strongest and most courageous person they knew. My friend conveyed to me the importance of listening and trusting my own intuition and being kind to myself. The inner struggle to recognise my self-worth continues to challenge me to this day. But I now understand that courage comes from learning to live with the trauma, rather than 'overcoming' it. The healing process is slow and non-linear but can be deeply transformative. Courage comes from discovering light from the darkness of traumatic experiences that can then become a powerful source of knowledge and knowing.

After longing to do so for over two decades, I finally found the courage to ignore the authoritative and dismissive voices of discouragement and to instead turn to a collaborative research agenda exploring the impact of gender-based violence on higher education access and participation. It has been awe-inspiring, rejuvenating and re-energising to learn from the accounts of hundreds of courageous students, and to mobilise the research as a platform to represent their collective knowledge, wisdom and insights. They have generously shared their stories in solidarity with other student survivors with the shared aim to generate understanding of how higher education matters in the intergenerational fight against gender-based violence. The student-participants strongly articulate their hope to make a difference to the lives of other women, and they want it to be known that the life chance to participate in higher education is crucial to their wellbeing, flourishing and capacity to give to others. One woman participating in the research puts it eloquently, explaining that, 'Education itself provides the freedom, focus and escape to a better future for women and children. It's not rocket science. Free education. Opportunity to thrive leads to contributing citizens. The hidden women numbers are huge.'[4]

*

Courage emerges from speaking truth to power. It comes from knowledge grounded in lived experience and the collective will to counter misrecognition and create solidarity and compassion. Powerful knowledge emerges from the courage to respond to the personal stories that illuminate what needs to change. Feminist, decolonial and anti-racist knowledge and practice are part of this process of care-full responsiveness. Learning from the student-participants has enabled me to see that recognising their collective knowledge and capacity is the key to eradicating gender-based violence and building sustainable, deep and meaningful forms of gender equality within and across all contexts of our lives. It is only through generating collective knowledge that transformative change for gender justice can happen – change rooted in the courage, recognition and value of knowing differently.

Prolonged Exposure—Lisa Collyer

AB, ABT, DV, SXM

Fifty-four. A woman in a drape dress signs books and smiles for the camera.

There's a box of books in my living room. I am on a grand tour of Europe, but there is nowhere I'd rather be right now than home. There's another box wrapped and beribboned, which I'll never open. It might be in my top drawer or at the back of my wardrobe. The note attached, which has yellowed with time, reads, *It's a gift of love.* It takes courage to hold love, even when I know it's just a wooden cube.

Fifty-one. A staff headshot of a woman wearing brick-red lipstick with ironed hair.

'I need an escape,' I tell my colleague and swivel my legs aside to allow her entry into the row of seats. There is no apparent danger, but I'm anxious to take flight. This position is the longest stretch I've been employed with one employer. I am a temporary teacher and must apply for my position each year. I request permanency, but the head of department reads flight risk in my foot-tapping tic.

Seventeen. A photobooth snapshot of two teenage girls pulling faces.

I lose my virginity in a caravan in the backyard of the duplex we are renting. When his thirty-year-old girlfriend finds out, she and her friend beat me up on the street on my way to work. I call out to a pedestrian for help, but he crosses the road. The mint linen top that I just finished sewing is now ripped. That night, my mother goes around to her house and sorts her out.

Five. A close-up of a wide-eyed schoolgirl in profile.
My mother comes to collect me from school. I am drawing bricks. We are moving interstate to South Australia. The house is left incomplete.

Thirteen. A polaroid of cousins in holy confirmation outfits in front of a double-storey brick house.
Our home in Corrimal, New South Wales, is the place we've lived the longest. I have best friends, but I always make new ones. We stay connected as penpals until correspondence peters out. We beg my father to stay put, but work is drying up where he labours in the blast furnace. And besides, he has a date with fate.

Fourteen. A polaroid of a girl stabbing a birthday cake with a knife. 'Don't touch the bottom or you'll never get married!' her family shrieks.
The morning light rouses me and I'm fleetingly hopeful. My mother shrinks. She barely eats and instead pops analgesics to dull the thud and the unknown man who shares her bed. By lunchtime, he's ranting. I am a slut at fourteen, although I've never been kissed. My mother is a slut because she wears blue eyeshadow. Now, my mother is in my bedroom, with her back against the door as he rants, 'Slut, slut, slut!' My mother implores me to 'never get married'. I make a vow that I never will.

Twenty-five. A slim woman poses in tie-dye against the door of a foreign place of worship.
A vase falls out of a station wagon and smashes into glazed fragments. I leave it and my friends behind. When I arrive in Byron Bay, all the accommodation is booked, but I refuse to budge until the tourism guide finds a surfer dude who has fold-out beds for rent. I remove my shoes and underwear and walk down the street in nothing but a slip-on frock. I meet P. It's not his real name but nor is mine. Reinvention becomes part of survival.

Thirteen. A teen sits on a red racer bike, in short shorts and a lollipop-striped singlet.
He likes his dinner on the table, on time. My mother knows his routine after his timber-yard job, where he labours to save money for the brickie, chippie or plasterer of our latest owner-build. We thought it was too cool when he bought a 250cc motorcycle.

Thirty-four. A Kodachrome of a padi field being irrigated at first light.
There's my bike in that box and I must trust that it will arrive on the internal flight from Ho Chi Minh City to Hanoi. Somehow, the chaos manifests in a bike frame and scattered parts on a hotel-room carpet. I burst into tears. I must prove myself.

Twenty-four. Friends in fancy dress, with red-eye, hold drinks and cigarettes.
My flatmates thoughtfully procure a St John's first-aid kit as my parting gift when I proclaim I'm off travelling. It's bulky, so I leave it in storage with all my belongings I'll never claim. My friends don't understand what it means to travel light.

Thirty-six. A long shot of a robber crab on a sandy beach.
When my freight arrives from Christmas Island, there are two items missing. My African djembe had to be quarantined or torched to cinders because of its animal skin, for a sum I could not afford. My aluminium bike arrives pedal-less. Is this stevedore vengeance on M.'s behalf?

Fifteen. A triptych of framed children hanging on an exposed-brick wall.
We stow a few belongings at the back of our wardrobes. We have luggage limits. There are three girls – fifteen, twelve, two – and one woman. She is thirty-four but already stoops. She drives us over the border from South Australia into New South Wales in a Holden Sunbird. When we stop for the night at a motel, we park out the back and close the drapes.

Sixteen. An overexposed driver's licence photo.
We live in a one-bedroom apartment in Merrylands, New South Wales. My older cousin takes me to a party, but I don't know how to mix my drinks. My sister feels sorry for me when my mother gives me a hiding after I vomit in the top bunk. The next day greets me with the smell of bacon.

Fifteen. A girl holds a baby on her bony hip.
We compartmentalise. Guilt only serves to delay and doubt. He's at the TAB placing a bet with his brothers, who sponge off his compo. We put our belongings in the boot. Books and clothes are what I take. We leave our bikes at Gran's in North Haven, South Australia. My mother leaves her wedding dress and a chicken defrosting on the kitchen bench, so he has something to eat that night.

At some point, men begin to make my skin crawl.

Thirteen. A school class photo of the year of 1982 wearing knee-length pleated skirts and white shirts.
I don't like schoolyard cliques. I have a best friend and a go-to set that I see out of school but during lunch, I work the yard. Today I will mix with this group, tomorrow that. I have no allegiance and get bored by internal chitchat.

It's difficult to trust *anyone*.

Thirty-three. A family stands by the side of the road while an athlete runs past holding the Olympic torch.
I take the phone off the hook because S. can't accept 'no'. When I reconnect it, he calls again. I take the phone off the hook for another week. It takes gumption to resist a man's pestering.

Fourteen. A girl stands by a man, who's under forty and leaning on a walking frame. He has a small scar on his head.
We all find ways to cope. My sister cuts us off, blinds closed, drinking red cordial while watching *The Exorcist*. My father's voice amplifies, and we all tense up. He smashes the phone with his bare fist. Now it hangs like a broken doll's head. My mother tries to placate him. I'm not sure what his brother said, but now he's sitting and sobbing and then begins to vomit. I make a cup with my hands to catch his spew.

Seventeen. A young woman in a white sales uniform with a perm.
I like sex. With his girlfriend out of the way, I go on a trip to J.'s place of work and loaf about in his caravan. I wear black lace. At this age, I know what it means to act out. When he proposes, I dry up and tell him to fuck off.

I can give in, but I choose not to. I refuse to ever care enough that I'll be trapped. Children weigh you down, so I abort. I refuse to perform the maternal role I was born to, and think of this as courage.

Thirty-one. Outside my bedroom window, a sheep I name Dolly grazes in next-door's paddock.
I get a professional job and buy my first car. I am a high school teacher, and they call me Miss Pits. It doesn't slow me down and it's difficult to settle. In my first year, I live in six different rentals. Eventually, I borrow five hundred dollars from my mother to put a deposit on a one-bedroom unit, and adopt a cat.

Thirty-nine. A woman with ripped abs poses in a hot-pink belly-dance costume.
After the collapse, I quit teaching and swear I'll never go back. The first month, I sit in the sun in the backyard listening to insect hum. My mother tells me, 'Put your hands in the dirt; that's how I got through your dad.' I take up hot composting and work as a temp.

Fifteen. An extended family of three generations sits morosely on maroon leather seats.
Dad has a black kangaroo inked on his right wrist, a coming-of-age identity. It was a tactic to assimilate after the post-war migration, and looked like his alien stamp upon entry. How unintentionally precise? A black kangaroo coat of arms, staking a counterclaim in a pecking order of sovereignty in so-called 'Australia'.

After the accident, he only remembers the distant past.

It's a typical rellie bash. I sit by my mum, who is bored shitless as usual, while the kids play out the back. My dad makes a memorable entrance, limping with his prosthetic gait. Although this time he's holding a loaded rifle cocked high on his shoulder and chortling. He places the muzzle against my nonna's head. I hold my breath and forget how to exhale.

Thirteen. A compact man sits with three children on a blue motorbike. One of the children is wearing an oversized red helmet.
Crash. Clunk … on metal and everything begins … to turn … eerily slowly. He … catapults, haloed. Thwack … unforgivingly … his head ricochets … back and forth, a basketball dribble before it settles and shuts down.

Thirteen. The front page of the newspaper depicts a burnt-out street and charred bush.
My dad is an alien creature. His brain swells – blue, violet and misshapen. Asleep in the intensive care unit, plastic tubes invade his nose, mouth and penis.

Fourteen. A young woman wears a jade boob-tube dress with a holy card tucked in the top.
A nurse appears and shoos us out so she can change his leg dressing. I am too slow and before the curtains close, the bloodied gauze is whipped off. I see the carcass-like chasm beneath the ragged edges.

Fifteen. A teenager with a plait poses in a pink-and-grey bubble skirt.
I, the laggard, spot the ground, step-by-step, a walking meditation, a scholastic scoliosis – a schoolgirl's homework load.

Fifteen. An autograph book reads: 'May your life be gentle and kind. Mrs Parry'
I start the new term, period one, in a rush of exhilaration as I enter the demountable for Free Dance. The teacher's chestnut hair hangs loose, as she invites me into the fold. Barefoot, I find a space to be close to Mrs Parry and her lacy cuffs ballooning out of her velvet vest festooned in brass. We rotate around her sun. 'Oh, to be an Isadorable!' The music engulfs me with its melancholic swing. I sway now and twirl, spotting her flowing hem. Embroidered motifs flash past as I spin and drop.

All the images spinning.
Thoop, thoop, thoop … whump! whump! whump!

The fluorescent tubes flicker, casting their patients in a ghoulish palette. The central ceiling fan thumps on each rotation. Laid back on starched sheets, shackled to prevent self-harm: I pity you. Where is my man of steel? My father reverts to baby, and I grow up, all at once.

He enters the bedroom. My mother finally breaks.

Some may wonder, what prompted us to leave? No-one ever asks, but I'll never stop running until this tale is told. Some may question the type of woman who ups and walks out on a broken man. This young woman, who was a girl. My dad should've died, but we needed to survive.

Some of us manage to move on better than most. But have I? My smile is armed, although my words pitter-patter consolation. I will not let anyone control me, and I know now, that all I am is the past.

Well, I ran! I made my family all run. Up and left while Dad was taking a punt on the gee-gees, looking for luck, which had well run its course. Pack your bags! Pack needs, not wants. Time is scarce. Space is at a premium. Clothes and books are all I need. Nothing's changed. He comes looking, of course, forever driving us underground. Shoulders stoop, heads slung low. Look left, look right; scan the platform before boarding. I never really shake that gait.

In ten years, he'd be dead, and my family could shed our fake identities, but fear holds fast, congealed behind painted masks, to outmanoeuvre danger.

Thirty-seven. A ragtag group of adults dressed in sequins and feather boas playing samba drums.
I ditch F. for another love tryst. A first date and the temporary status of M. tempts in eco slogans that blare 'gentle hippie freak that makes me cum'. Perhaps I'll learn to trust this one. Every day this takes courage.

I watch a couple in a cafe drinking tea and call it love.

Forty-five. A sextet plays free jazz.
Can I ever be free of the past? He encourages me to connect – when I am here to disconnect. I've been feeling too much lately and I'd like to feel a little bit less. What could I say that hadn't been said before? 'I'm sorry.' I left the painted stone on your tomb, but I didn't have the guts to speak to you, because seeing the photo of you on the headstone made me cry.

Fifty-two. A Google Earth image of a brick home with a quarter-acre block of grass.
Heat islands of brick and tile jockey, cheek-by-jowl in new suburbs, in the great green class divide. We buy a quarter-acre block then tie the knot. The courage to settle is like pinning down a tightly sprung jill-in-the-box.

Forty-five. A woman in khaki workwear stands in front of a sandpaper wattle that lights up the blue sky.
On my back, I watch clouds convey a new weather system's drift. The ants twitch to the commute. My gloves wear through to bare fingers. Dirt fills cut nails. Back to work. On knees. I lift the foliage and knuckle down to the perseverance of couch grass, digging deep and excavating extensions – a knowing they'll return. A ground spider flees, and I learn to lay roots, and exhale.

Fifty. A woman in Tiffany sunglasses squats in front of a black gravestone.
I've a husband now. Last time I visited Dad's grave I hollered at him. Now rows of gravestones buckle and resist, but we eventually stumble across him. I kneel and look at Dad and take a photograph to send to my sisters. I feel silly talking to Dad, but I tell him I'm sorry. It wasn't something I did, forgiveness. I touch his face but am unsure how long to stay. My husband takes a photo of me. Should I smile?

The Ring of Knowledge – Paola Magni

DTH

I recall a story from my high school days that has always stuck with me. There was a legend from the toughest school in the city that one day, a teacher assigned an essay in class with the simple title, 'What is courage?' To everyone's surprise, one student completed the entire essay by writing just one word: 'This.'

That story fascinated me, leaving me to wonder if I could ever be as bold as that person. Would I ever summon the audacity to take risks, do the unexpected, and stand up for myself?

I was born on a cold December night in the north of Italy, to loving, hardworking parents. We lived in a small, cosy city apartment. In my bedroom I had toys, a little play kitchenette and a big mat with bright colours that became my playground. Life was simple, and worry-free. But how does someone who grows up without worries become courageous?

Daydreaming adventures of my favourite Disney characters, I would use the colours of the mat to imagine being a mermaid in the ocean, a lost princess in the woods or a pixie better at friendship than Tinkerbell. But my mat adventures were never a dinnertime topic. It was always about school, homework, friends – the routine. Everything was fine. I was a good kid, good at school, kind and nice. Mum and Dad were happy, and the teacher was happy. But deep down, something was missing.

The feeling was like a smouldering fire beneath the ashes.

Maybe in another time or in a parallel universe, this feeling would have taken me to jump on a ship, join a pirate crew and explore the world, or cut my long blonde hair and become a musketeer. I remember the Mardi Gras in which my mum agreed to let me dress up as D'Artagnan; I still smile, thinking how amazing the feeling was of that horrible red lycra cape and how happy I was to wield that plastic sword.

I had the same smile every Friday night when there was the weekly episode of *Superquark*, two uninterrupted hours of documentaries that today we can watch at any time on the Discovery Channel. It was the time of the week in which I could walk in the savannah on tippy toes so as not to wake up the lions, discover the jelly creatures in the Mariana Trench, find new stars watching from the Paranal Observatory.

Ever since I can remember, the disappointment of receiving another Barbie for Christmas instead of a ticket to Sweden to see the midnight sun was almost overwhelming. It must be why I am still not a Christmas person ... But luckily, the Holy Christening was coming, and I could ask for something special. Too many houses in front of ours for a telescope, building rules against pets, but plenty of space on my desk for a microscope. And you cannot use a microscope without a lab coat – so my mum got an old one from the janitor at her school – and without glasses: an old pair of my dad's with no lenses, with an elastic band at the back to hold them in place on my still-little head.

I was finally ready to sail the sea to different types of adventures, my adventures, even if in a few square millimetres.

*

Throughout the years, I put all kinds of things on microscope slides, from drops of rain to tears, blood and tomato sauce, ants, seeds, pieces of paper, dust and flour. Sometimes, it was magical, and sometimes it was frustrating because I had no clue that I was supposed to use special colours to make certain things visible. Nobody around me was able to support my learning journey – my mum was a special-needs teacher for kids, my dad a hotel manager – so I found myself in the local library with the librarian questioning why I was not visiting the children's section that was 'more appropriate' for a girl like me. My favourite book was *King Solomon's Ring*, written by Nobel Prize laureate Konrad Lorenz for his studies on animal behaviour. The title referred to the legendary ring that gave King Solomon the power to speak to animals – my biggest dream.

Luckily, things improved in high school because a teacher recognised my willingness to learn and gave me the opportunity to help prepare classes for older students during the weekend. With an old aquarium found in the basement, he even helped me make a 'pond' and breed water fleas.

It wasn't a surprise that at the end of the university orientation day, I settled on the course of Natural Sciences. If you have a pot plant, a biologist will focus on the trunk and the leaves, while a geologist will focus on the materials of the pot and the soil ... but a natural scientist will be interested in the biology of the leaves and the chemistry of the soil, and at the same time will think about the changes that occur because of the surrounding environment and the actions of humans. For a natural scientist, the science of life and the science of earth are connected by never-ending dynamics in which humans also play an important part.

Nature was my profound love, my calling. But I never imagined where answering this call was going to take me.

*

I was returning home from field research in Kazakhstan, in charge of collecting green toads for a population genetics project thanks to a prestigious international scholarship. While it was a once-in-a-lifetime experience, for the first time in many years, I was unhappy because I couldn't find purpose in my study. Again, something was missing. Lots of data on paper, but emptiness in my heart.

Courage, bravery and craziness overlap sometimes, and I decided to withdraw from the project and give up the scholarship – not the greatest move considering the general lack of funds for natural scientists. And why not add another unit to my study plan, entomology – the science that studies insects?

Insects had never been my thing. Too small or too big, definitely too annoying, not particularly interactive, with a lifespan too short or too long to be an interesting 'pet' to observe on a daily basis, and dietary requirements that would have quickly earned me an eviction notice from my parents' house. But insects are the essence of nature. They are everywhere, their bodies are adapted to live in the desert or in a glacier; their life cycles can be so different that adults and offspring often live in different places and eat different things so that they don't compete with each other. And nature dictates the speed of their life cycle: shorter when it's warm, and longer when it's cold. They can even enter a stand-by mode for years if the environmental situation isn't ideal for their survival. They are able to colonise, predate, parasitise, pollinate, bring diseases and clean wounds. It's unbelievable that entomology was an elective subject in a natural sciences course.

During the first entomology class, I learned that insects are mostly studied because they are beautiful, like typical butterflies or beetles; useful, like bees; or dangerous because they bring pathogens, like some species of mosquitoes. Interestingly, while some entomologists have a specific interest in certain groups, lots of insects are not studied at all.

There was a moment of silence, just before the class was finished and some people started packing their bags, when the professor added, 'Oh, and in the last few years, a group of scientists has been interested in using knowledge about insects for criminal investigation.'

I am not sure if anyone else noted that remark, but that sentence glued me to the chair. I am almost sure that my jaw dropped while I was thinking about the meaning of that sentence in terms of the nature surrounding a crime scene and the role that insects could have there.

It was the beginning of 2001, and the popular *CSI: Crime Scene Investigation* was yet to be released in Italy. The closest crime drama we had was *Murder, She Wrote*, with Jessica Fletcher dealing with all sorts of suspicious cases. However, in no episode did insects play a role, neither for victims who were alive at the beginning of the episode nor for those found long after the murder. In reality, this would be unlikely. In 1668 Francesco Redi, one of the fathers of natural sciences and experimental biology, proved that maggots are not spontaneously generated by flesh, but come from eggs laid by flies on rotten meat shortly after exposure to the environment. In the best conditions this process can take as little as a few minutes. I'm sure scriptwriters knew this, but they didn't let these gruesome details interfere with their storylines. Though, surprisingly, ignoring the insects could have turned some of Jessica Fletcher's successful cases into miscarriages of justice instead.

And the question in my head was: Is there anyone in Italy who takes care of these Sherlock-bugs, providing them with the opportunity to unveil the true story behind a criminal event?

There wasn't, really. No natural scientists were taking the responsibility of translating the key left by nature at the crime scene, leaving many questions unsolved for the justice system and for the families of victims.

Two of the victims of the Italian serial killer the Monster of Florence, for example, were found dead in Tuscany after going missing on a camping trip, with a report saying lots of maggots had infested the bodies, but they were not used to provide information to the investigators.

Similarly, eighteen-year-old Serena Mollicone was found hidden in a bush with lots of maggots inside the plastic bag that was covering her face. At the time of her murder, Serena and I were pretty much the same age.

A natural scientist could have helped with the Mollicone investigation, starting with the identification of the species and the collection of the environmental data. To an untrained eye, maggots and flies may all look the same, but there are several different species that have different habits, behaviours and growth rates. Temperature, humidity, rainfall and presence of toxicological substances can all affect the estimation of their age, which in turn provides an indication of the time of death. Insects found in association with the body of a victim – whether human or animal – can represent the sole evidence of the presence of drugs or poisons, or can provide clues regarding the potential relocation of the body from a primary crime scene to the location where it was discovered. They may even contain foreign DNA, belonging to individuals who interacted with the victim around the time of death.

A maggot has mouth hooks to break flesh, a fly has a spongy proboscis to suck liquid, and they both make noise with the movement of their body or their wings. The only way for them to 'talk' in the witness box is for someone to wear King Solomon's signet ring and translate what their presence and activity mean at the crime scene.

That day during the entomology class, by chance, the professor inadvertently pointed out to me where the ring was. Like a stubborn treasure hunter who refuses to take no for an answer, I managed to find it – yet possessing the ring and mastering its power are entirely different matters.

*

Once again, I found myself in a situation where nobody around me was able to support my learning journey. But this time, I was old enough to rely on my savings earned from various odd jobs – from dog walking and school tutoring to bartending – to seek help. I travelled around Europe and the United States to wear this ring comfortably. I met with the best forensic scientists in the world and took the courage to ask questions in my broken English to learn more. I knocked on many doors, offering my support with a pretty weird pitch: 'When you have a case, I can come to collect the maggots and, in a few days, I can provide you with information that might be useful for your investigation ...'

Slowly, I realised that King Solomon's ring meant much more than a relationship with the creatures at the scene. The investigation is a complex process involving many people of different roles and backgrounds – lawyers, judges, police, pathologists, toxicologists and the citizens on the jury. Throughout the investigation of a criminal case, it's not the scientist against the judge, but what the lawyers and the jury understand of what the forensic expert says, that can drive the case in one direction or another. To make it shine, King Solomon's ring had to be able to break complex concepts into a language that everyone could understand.

Ten years after Serena Mollicone's death, I was asked to be part of the team that reopened and re-analysed her case. The information stored by the insects, still present in her clothes – which had been kept by the police – was finally used to reconstruct the events surrounding her disappearance. To this day, the insect clues remain the only ones used for estimating her time of death, and which led to the crushing of certain people's alibis.

*

These days, a knowledgeable and passionate young woman at the forefront of her field might become an influencer or an entrepreneur. But a few years ago, being a scientist in a niche field simply meant not being able to find a job.

For several years after leaving my parents' house, I led a triple life. In the mornings, I taught maths and science at a secondary school, leveraging my specialisation in science education earned during my natural science degree. In the afternoons, I conducted research in the basement of the chemistry department. And when needed, I worked on forensic cases and provided police training. It was a struggle to make ends meet, financially, physically and emotionally.

One day, during a morning break at school, I found fifteen missed calls on my mobile phone. The police were desperately trying to reach me regarding a high-profile homicide case that required my expertise. Tears welled in my eyes as I realised I couldn't leave school immediately.

Two days later, I found myself five-hundred kilometres away from home. The body of a young woman had been discovered on the shore of a lake, with her boyfriend as the prime suspect. However, the pathologist claimed it was a natural death, and there was not sufficient evidence to refute the young man's alibi that he hadn't been at the lake with her. Another 'no' in this case was the absence of insects, as was the absence of the body from the scene. While the young woman's body had been moved, nature could still tell a story through another piece of evidence – the lake's plankton.

Like an inverted evolution process, in the years following my degree, I further developed my expertise, transitioning from terrestrial to aquatic environments. However, I ensured that I was proficient in both realms, recognising that crimes and crime scenes can occur in any form, shape, and location, and nature permeates every single one.

For the first time in my country, the court considered confirming the boyfriend's alibi by testing his clothes for plankton. If he hadn't been at the lake, no plankton should have been found on his clothes. It required numerous jars of water, extensive clothing samples and hundreds of hours working in a laboratory in the basement of the University of Turin to compile a report indicating which clothes tested positive for plankton, matching the specific plankton assemblage of the lake.

These findings triggered a chain reaction of case reopenings, new autopsies and a compelling case against the boyfriend – ultimately resulting in his arrest and imprisonment for the homicide.

After the high-profile case and the extensive media coverage it received, I truly believed that I might finally secure a job. However, that wasn't the case. I was told: You are not a biologist, you are not a chemist, you are not a police officer, you are not a pathologist. You are great, but you are 'not' (enough? in the right box? with the right contacts?) and Italy is 'not' (ready? the right place?). Interestingly, though, my professional profile was eccentric enough to inspire the creation of a new character for the Italian version of *CSI*: *RIS Delitti Imperfetti*. I became the muse and scriptwriter for the forensic entomology expert on the police team, finally allowing me to contribute to show business by accurately depicting the role of maggots at crime scenes.

*

Moving overseas by myself wasn't easy, but it felt like the right decision. I seized the opportunity of a scholarship application in Australia and positioned myself in front of a metaphorical sliding door. If I received the scholarship, I would move forward; if not, I would close the chapter on my science dream. And I was resolute about that.

A few weeks after winning the scholarship, I snuck out of Italy, leaving a letter for my grandmother, apologising for the need to be myself.

In the last few years, life hasn't been easy. I've had to readjust to a new country and lifestyle, navigate a new job, embrace a new partner, and experience the profound joy and challenge of becoming a mother – twice. Despite the geographical change, some interpersonal issues remain consistent. I've learned the hard way how to choose my battles wisely and not let things I cannot control affect me.

Amidst these challenges, I found my community – a group of people with whom I can comfortably sit at a table, share stories, make plans and support each other's journeys.

Science, nature and discovery define me. Taking the responsibility of using knowledge for the greater good is my calling. I sought adventure and courage, and last year, I was honoured with the knighthood of my home country.

Embracing myself, trusting my knowledge and courage, breaking stereotypes and making statements that can change the course of justice have so far been the most difficult but also the most rewarding things I've accomplished.

It all came together the day I found myself in court, with an old judge asking me a direct question: 'In your expert opinion, what is the reconstruction of the event?' Without hesitation, I replied, 'This.'

Beyond 'Waste' and In/fertility: Courage and Poetry in the Heart of Rot—Nadia Rhook

MCS, PRG

'I wasted time, and now doth time waste me'
– Shakespeare, *Richard II*, 1595

In 1789, an English woman, Susannah Mortimer, was charged with stealing a sheep, sentenced to transportation, and shipped across the world to Eora Country. During the passage, she gave birth to a daughter she named after herself. In their very fleshy, gendered lives, Susannah mother and daughter were caught up in a project to redress the gender imbalance in the fledgling new colony and to secure possession of Indigenous lands by boosting the colonist population. Mother and daughter soon landed in a place where white men were hungry for the next delivery of rations, weapons and women, and where sovereign parents had been caring for their children for over one thousand generations already. Three hundred years later, living on the other side of the continent called 'Australia', on Whadjuk boodja, I underwent IVF to become something called 'mother', and my family and I joined Susannah in a story where reproduction is far too wondrous and far too political for comfort. This essay is about how I grew a determination to live beyond ideas that a woman's value lies in biological motherhood, an attempt to let flourish the courage to live and be beyond colonial binaries of improvement and waste.

*

I wanted to be a mother for as long as I can remember, and I wanted to be a published writer for almost as long. 'Book then baby' was my mantra while I finished my PhD, obtained a book contract and sought full-time employment. Soon after I turned thirty, with the book's completion promising, my partner and I decided it was time to try to have a child. We committed to the process of conception, which was to commit to a closer observation of my body. I downloaded an app to track my cycles and inspected my body's fluids. Despite our carefully timed lovemaking, my periods continued.

Time was now measured by absence. No pregnancy. No child. No chance to take advantage of the relative job security I'd finally, fortunately accrued. Perhaps I was too stressed? I avoided strenuous exercise. I tried to put on weight and did. My partner stopped eating processed meats. I don't recall how long passed like this. Three years? I guess the number of days or months or years is a blur for a reason, the mind's attempt to smooth out the harshness of subjecting ourselves to incessant measurements and their accompanying jabs of lack. I do remember that eventually, my GP referred me to a fertility specialist. Soon after, I got a job opportunity in another city, and we agreed to postpone the process. Back to square one.

Once in Boorloo (Perth), we were eventually referred to a clinic. We took our seats. Nervous. Excited. The doctor showed me a graph with an exponential curve, showing me that as I was almost thirty-five, my fertility was dropping away. It looked like a cliff. All terror and sudden plummets toward a reality that would not end in more life, let alone with the exquisite sight of a baby curling its tiny hand around my maternal finger.

*

During the years of trying to become pregnant, I navigated a grief that felt uncannily complex. My grandmother and then my former supervisor and mentor lost their lives to the same uncommon cancer. A friend suddenly lost her partner. A library staff member had a heart attack while I was convening a panel in the library and, shortly after, passed away. So many of my colleagues had passed or were unwell that I was asked to organise Open Day at the institution I worked because, as my manager put it in bluntly Foucauldian terms, 'biopower is down'. What was more, not all of these deaths were equal. The length of one's life, I was (re)learning, was unjustly shaped by history – by the many and miscellaneous colonial systems and forces that meant some people had a greater chance at longevity than others. The tension felt unspeakable. How can I put my effort into creating another (white settler) life while others are unjustly losing theirs?

*

Like many attuned to inequality, I understood by this time that colonial racial capitalism values productivity that places white profit and white life as supreme. Eighteenth- and nineteenth-century English land laws strategically labelled sacred First Nations' Country as unproductive 'waste land'. Developed in the Great Britain and through the English colonisation of Ireland, these laws were adapted as the British colonised First Nations land in so-called Australia and underwrote the laying down of mammoth stretches of irrigation channels, designed to make more productive land.[1] An extract of an 1817 Bill reads:

> If Commons Moor or Waste Lands in their present state yield little profit, but if they are divided, then the

> lands can be Divided and Inclosed to His Majesty, and to several Persons with Rights of Common.[2]

It doesn't take much research to find that as inequalities of race register in the treatment of land, so do inequalities of sex and gender register in bodies. In her trailblazing work *A Vindication of the Rights of Woman*, Mary Wollstonecraft, a mother of Western feminism, put forth the argument of women's emancipation in a patriarchal society, which essentially required women to just 'procreate and rot'.[3] This patriarchal use of women has settler-colonial implications. In the story of Susannah it was painfully clear to me that the same logic used to valuate lands as in/fertile is also used to valuate women's bodies. The colony desires convict women like my ancestor Susannah for their reproductive abilities. In short, while First Nations' land was valuable for its ability to grow crops, white women were valuable for their corporeal ability to grow white settler families.

*

And so, as I counted my privileges and daydreamed about adoption, those eighteenth- and nineteenth-century English land laws haunted me. They now seemed a comment not only on the utility of land but that of my body too. The word 'waste' wrapped its weightless fingers around the neck of my childless life.

I didn't, during these years, perform poems that talked about infertility, except for one. While googling 'waste land' I stumbled across a poem by well-known English poet T.S. Eliot. I played with his poem and rewrote its famously ambiguous stance on colonialism in more firmly anti-colonial terms. I called my poem, tongue-in-cheek, after the song written by Solomon Linda and recorded by The Weavers in 1951.

In the Jungle

Whose law rules in the jungle?
I don't know, but it's not mine

Leaves, too, reach for the sky
They, neither, are a stranger to light
These leaves shall never be called
A waste land

Waste as in barren as in uncultivated
Waste as in we'd better use it so we can keep it/...

The roots.../
Stretch their bended brown limbs
From the dirt to the place
Where the canopy begins

What are the roots?
They funnel the fear of thirst
From the moist bed to the leaves
And the leaves are no stranger
To the sky

Dear Mr Eliot
This land was not a waste land
The law of this land was wasted on you[4]

Later, I would learn my intuition about the poem's relevance to my story was on point. It turns out that Eliot's 'Waste Land' is based on a fertility myth about a kingdom left barren when a curse is placed upon its king by way of a castration wound.

The Fisher King fishes and fishes in his land without yield as he guards the Holy Grail.[5] The story of the Fisher King links the king's health to that of the land.[6] In this ancient turned imperial story, infertility is the awful stuff of tragedy and demise.

*

There is, I believe, a courage involved in knowing from the inside out the structures of colonialism that permeate our society. But it was not identifying the waste/productivity binary per se that gave me courage, but rather the embodied performance of poetry about it. Standing on stages across Naarm (Melbourne) and then Boorloo, my voice amplified by microphones, my body silhouetted by bright lights, I came into a new relationship with 'waste'. At the phrase about the branches, I held my hand high and twisted it – the shape of a branch growing leaves. At the word 'uncultivated', I held my stomach tenderly – respect for my empty womb. More than once, I saw a flash of recognition in the eyes of someone in the audience. They felt it. The yearning. The absence. I held onto these flashes of recognition and allowed myself to imbue these small moments with immeasurable gravitas. While colonialism was inviting me to live according to the logic of waste/productivity, in poetry I inhabited a world of visceral understanding. Poets see straight through the cushion of metaphors to the pain beneath.

*

Meanwhile, my thoroughly biological issue of fertility continued: a question that lived under my bed, a monster of a childless future. The science was clear. To increase my chances of becoming pregnant, I had to relax. This was challenging. To risk an IVF cycle was to risk its failure, or even worse, miscarriage. In order to create this courage, I needed a comfort deeper than I could intellectualise or dream.

One morning, walking to my regular cafe in Walyalup (Fremantle), my eye was caught by a medley of colours near my feet. I stopped. Leaves and petals floating in a puddle. In the process of transforming, from solid to liquid. Something loosened in my chest. Something that made me, opposite to Wollstonecraft, enjoy the possibilities of rot.

I began to habitually pause to behold the beauty of rotting things, caressing with my eyes the fact of decay. The day before I went under a general anaesthetic and a doctor scraped my eggs from my ovaries, I:

> … smell the footpath while I walk gas, blossom, petrol
> /…
> rotting leaves my closest comfort stews of life bubbling
> on the footpath
> fertilising the city just in case she's a womb, or wishes
> to bloom
> try to walk this street like it's a place where the nectar
> hasn't yet ended and the rot's already begun[7]

Rituals, writes poet and anthropologist Michael Jackson, are a way of transforming lived experiences of the world and a strategy for gaining control in the face of hardships.[8] I began stopping to take a photo of any rotting thing. A way to become more intimate with the future's intense uncertainties.

*

Another visit to the specialist. Another look at the exponential fertility curve and discussion of options. We finally commit to the first cycle. If it goes well, it will culminate in the implantation of an embryo into my womb.

I decided to give these petals more attention. To give something attention, poetry had taught me, was to give it power. Whenever I saw petals, I sank my eyes into them. Much later, I wrote a poem about the history of this flower, how it was named after Louis-Antoine de Bougainville, but his assistant and lover, Jeanne Baret, probably saw this plant before he did. Baret is often remembered as 'the first European woman to travel the globe'.[9] Because she was an expert in botany at a time when women's intellectual authority was not recognised, she was compelled to flatten her breasts with linen bandages to pass as a man.

I invite you, now, to see that there is a queer sense running through this story, if you, if I, am willing to see it as that. A disillusionment with the heteronormative expectations around conception and child-bearing that contributed to my internalised shame around infertility. A knowing that reproduction and sex are not the same thing. A wanting to unsettle gender binaries. A desire for ways of being and creating that flourish beyond binaries.

Bougainvillea flowers connect with the history of a woman who had to suppress part of herself (her chest and her authority) in order to fulfil her desire to sail and produce knowledge about the world. I hoped the reader might read deeper meanings into this story, as I did. No matter what we want, women are rewarded for flattening something of our multidimensionality as we attempt to navigate a world that tries to keep us at a distance from our power, which is a world that tries to irrigate the dominance and authority of man out of the submissiveness and innocence of woman.

*

We might reflect a little longer on all those things most likely to be treated wastefully. A waste of time. A waste of space. A waste of a life. A waste of talent. A waste of money. Let's be crystal clear about the idea beneath each of these adages. To waste all these things is to disrespect the capital you could have gained had you acted according to the logic and demands of colonialism. Land, bodies, time, space, money. All good while used.

*

The embryo becomes a foetus. The foetus becomes a body with strong legs that kick my body's stretched walls, a body that flips like a seal trapped inside me in the evenings.

After going for a swim, I see a drop of blood in my bathers. I call the hospital. Come in, they urge.

Tests. Scans. Questions.

The body inside me is no longer growing as fast as the doctors expect. I'm induced. Another injection. There are no flowers in the white-walled, fluorescent-lit room, not a single petal. Bunches of flowers don't arrive until after a baby is outside of you and the work of reproduction is celebrated as complete.

The contractions are fierce. My bones have not had enough chance to stretch and loosen. During labour, my baby's heartbeat drops. Uncertainty blooms obscenely. Will he live? My contractions rock me so violently they struggle to administer the epidural. Finally, I'm still and the needle finds my spine between contractions. Hours pass. It's not time to push yet. I get a fever. Will I live? A tunnel that funnels energy to another place, to death. It opens as I scream. My screams run along death's spine. I pass into a limitless realm.

Eventually, I'm wheeled to the operating table just in case they need to do an emergency C-section. My body is cut open and stitched, slowly, together.

A ball of life is placed on my chest.

Wonder. Joy untellable. Hot tears of hotter relief.

You're here. You're here.

I read him a poem the first morning of his life, and the mornings after.

He will be born, not into productivity, but into ritual and poetic moments that stretch and warp with abundance.

*

I've written this essay over the course of months, having recently moved from Whadjuk boodja to live in Naarm again, the city on Kulin Country where I was born. And so, I've written this essay as a settler inhabiting a space between migrant and local, strangeness and familiarity, as a self that has left parts behind and is finding a (re)new(ed) one. Doubt has diverted me from completing this story, far too much like an irrigation pipe laying courage-siphoning tracks through my aqueous, muddy mind. Am *I* deserving to be called a 'woman of courage'? Is finding a new perspective on in/fertility and IVF really a courage worth writing of, in these days of climate change and genocide and heartbreak? Then, I remember that climate change is in part a result of the systems of mass-scale irrigation that are having devastating environmental and social consequences, and I quickly clamber out of this channel of thought. It is, after all, a settler-colonising mindset. In my core now, I know that rot is a process unto its glorious process. Rot was, is, a transformation. Sweet and rancid, delicious and poisoning, a rendering of perfection superfluous. Rot, like IVF and life, is not something with clear beginnings and endings. It is a liminality. A petal already fallen but not yet earth. A nourishing decay turning gradually into compost. The very change of change. Change beyond the stultifying binaries of waste/productivity. Change that breaks free of irrigation channels to flow and circle through time. A struggle to separate a self from the systems ruining the earth and its peoples. A gradual honesty. A beautiful unknown.

I hoped, and hope, that my poetry expresses a solidarity with queer experiences of becoming a parent. Is IVF a queer experience, if only in a structural sense of separating sex from reproduction? Of course, plenty of straight people go through IVF and stay straight. But for me, something about this closer relationship with non-normativity made me want to not only better understand gender and sexuality, but to embrace the queerness sprouting, or perhaps resprouting, green shoots of liberation inside of me. To refuse binaries of waste/productivity now feels like entering a paradigm of abundance and ecology both anti-colonial and queer.[10]

And I will take my ears with me
And leave you, Sir, to wander in your waste land
And say goodnight, goodnight
Sweet petals sweet rotting stories
Goodnight[11]

On Breaking Out of Our Shells
—Cynthia Dearborn

HMP

As a child I rarely spoke, especially not at school. Between difficulties at home and my family's frequent moves – country to country as well as state to state, which meant I was constantly the new kid – I retreated into myself. 'She needs to come out of her shell,' a concerned school principal said of me when I was eleven, a comment I found maddening because if I'd known how to come out of my shell, I would have. People called me shy; I saw myself that way too, but in hindsight, I'd say I was scared. I never could have guessed that I'd grow up to become an activist, academic and author, that speaking out would be central to my life's work.

I don't think of myself as a particularly courageous person. But I vowed at the age of twenty-four not to let my life be limited by timidity and fear. So, I've had to be inventive, finding different ways of summoning the courage to speak out, to express my thoughts and experiences in public settings – especially in situations where what I have to say is unwelcome or speaking up at all could be dangerous.

*

December 1983. A packed courtroom in Kent, Washington, on the outskirts of Seattle; television crews waiting outside. I'd been charged with criminal trespass for entering a federal security area – the Boeing Aerospace Center, where cruise missiles were being made. I was about to deliver my opening argument, having opted to forgo a lawyer and represent myself; I didn't want anybody twisting my words, misrepresenting my reasons.

When my name was called, I rose and walked to the front of the room in my borrowed clothes, which I thought looked more 'respectable' (read: feminine) than the things I usually wore. Having been sworn in, I turned to acknowledge the judge, then the jurors, then the prosecutor, my four codefendants and their two lawyers, then the audience of spectators, including other activists from the Puget Sound Women's Peace Camp and, in the back row, my father, his balding head a beacon above the others.

Raised in a military family, I was used to keeping my opinions to myself. As a schoolkid I would sit in classroom after classroom in silence (even when called on, even when I knew the answer), and at the Peace Camp I would sit through meeting after meeting, listening to the ideas and strategies flying past me, forming and refining my own views, but far too timid to share them with others. This is why my opening argument at the trial was a watershed moment for me. I was going public with my core beliefs, my audacious hopes for a future free of nuclear weapons.

I unfolded my notes. I cleared my throat. I caught a glimpse of my dad's nervous smile. This is part of what I said:

> You're going to be hearing testimony that at times will be difficult to listen to. There will be strong words, there will be hard facts, and there will be photographs. So I'd like to ask you each to summon the courage

> to open not only your ears, but your minds and your hearts, to what we have to say.

As I continued my speech, which was about the urgency of averting nuclear war (the USA had begun sending first-strike, nuclear-tipped cruise missiles to Europe despite mass protests there), I could feel myself being changed by the experience even as it was unfolding. I could feel the audience absorbing my words. Though it was my first brush with the law, I felt in command of that courtroom. I knew that if the jury found us guilty and the judge imposed the maximum sentence, I'd lose my liberty for an entire year – as well as my job, my livelihood, my apartment, and probably my lover – but I felt calm, sure of myself in a way I rarely did.

Over the course of the trial, which went on for four days (complete with media circus), I discovered a simple way to conjure the courage I needed in the moment I needed it. I simply pictured someone I knew through the Peace Camp, someone whose work, or whose words, I'd found bold, courageous, generous; and I channelled that energy, drew it through my own body, breathed it in as fuel. The woman who started a neighbourhood clinic for those who couldn't afford a doctor; the woman who organised a human shield from the parking lot to the doorway of an abortion clinic, to protect the women coming to the clinic from the anti-abortionists who'd scream abuse at them and try to block their access; the woman trying to safeguard young runaways and sex workers from the Green River Killer, who was still at large and who preyed on these populations. Ordinary, extraordinary women surrounded me; inspiration was mine for the taking.

The verdict was announced, the sentencing hearing set. Three of us did jail time and two of us did not (I did not). We Peace Campers wrote a book called *We Are Ordinary Women:*

A Chronicle of the Puget Sound Women's Peace Camp, which includes my opening statement.[1] Though by now the spine of my copy is tattered and the pages loose, I keep it near my desk as a reminder of my Peace Camp experience and the many things it taught me, including ways of thinking about courage.

Courageousness is often thought of as a personality trait that one either possesses or lacks. But I find it useful to think of courage as an energy, a fluid force, a boundless collective reservoir that surrounds us all and can be tapped at will.

*

April 1993. A fancy hotel in Atlanta, Georgia. I'd flown in to be a panellist at the seven-thousand-strong international convention of TESOL, Teachers of English to Speakers of Other Languages. Shortly before I was to step on stage, I was checking messages sent to me via the convention's Intranet system (a novelty at that time). I clicked open a message from a convention participant whose name I did not know.

I read it. Re-read it. Then discreetly scanned my surroundings. Nothing ominous: just people milling about, perusing the program, their tote bags bearing the convention theme, *Designing Our World*.

I turned to Lisa, my friend and colleague, at the monitor next to mine and asked quietly, 'Did you get a death threat?'

We clicked through our remaining messages. Three each from convention participants whom we did not know, declaring their intent to kill us if we spoke as planned at our groundbreaking panel 'From Silence to Celebration: Lesbians and Gays in ESL.'[2]

I glanced at my watch. We had to decide what to do, and fast.

Lisa and I skimmed the hostile messages again. *Gay people don't belong in the classroom. Gay people are sick in the head. Gay people are evil. Gay people don't deserve to live.* All views

I had heard before – but never with a death threat attached, one lobbed directly at me by someone who was currently in the vicinity and knew exactly which building and room I'd be in, and when.

This was the early 90s. Politicians received death threats, celebrities, controversial authors like Salman Rushdie. But a language teacher? It seemed bizarre to be killed for a conference talk – but not unthinkable. LGBTQ rights was a hot-button topic worldwide. Homophobic attacks were rampant. Same-sex marriage was forbidden in every country in the world; and in some, being gay was punishable by death. All three of us panellists openly identified as gay or lesbian and had been urging our TESOL colleagues to acknowledge and engage with the real-world realities of sexual diversity. Teachers' responses had often been dismissive and disapproving, but this level of hostility was new to us.

As Lisa and I rushed to our designated conference room, we considered our options. Should we tell someone or keep it to ourselves? Where in this maze of buildings swarming with out-of-towners (like us) could we find somebody to tell, and in a hurry? Would our panel be cancelled, would the work we'd been doing to reach teachers internationally all be for naught, the momentum of our nascent movement lost? Or would whoever we told shrug us off, call us 'fucking dykes' under their breath? Because when people heard the name of our panel, we never knew what reaction we'd get.

We updated the other panellist and scanned the crowd. A few familiar faces, most unknown. No security in sight, no hotel staff. No outside moderator – just me. We blinked at each other. 'I'm fine to go on,' Jim said. 'We've worked so hard for this. But Cynthia, I'll leave it up to you.' Lisa looked at me and said, 'Me too.'

I felt conflicted. I'd experienced enough physical violence to know I didn't want any more of it, and I certainly didn't want to die a martyr for a cause. But if we let ourselves be scared into silence, we'd be perpetuating the very thing we were trying to change: the silencing of LGBTQ voices – and I'd witnessed first-hand the harm this inflicted and the limits it imposed on learning.

My personal circumstances factored into my decision-making too. I could take risks that people who were parents, guardians, or caregivers perhaps could not. Also, when I had told my mother, ten years before, that I was a lesbian, she had disowned me and hadn't spoken to me since. It was her glaring absence from my life, the ache of it, the injustice of it, that drove my efforts to make language classes more welcoming of queer learners and teachers.

I stepped up to the podium. Jim and Lisa took their seats beside me. I spoke into the mic. 'Welcome, everyone,' I said, my arms outstretched in a gesture of embrace, 'to the twenty-seventh annual lesbian, gay, bisexual, transgender and straight TESOL Convention!' That drew laughter from the crowd.

I briefly considered mentioning the death threats but decided against it, recalling advice that seasoned peace activists had given me a decade earlier: voice your own arguments, not those of your opponents; don't let them use you as their mouthpiece. I wanted to use my valuable minutes to carve out new possibilities: a vision of classrooms, and staff rooms, and curricula, and journals, and conferences, as spaces in which people of all sexual identities could be seen and heard and flourish.

I flashed on the advice I often gave my students when they were nervous about speaking: focus on your message, not your nerves; focus on what you want to say, not the judgements of others.

Our panel was extremely well received. Part of me remained on high alert throughout our presentation, and the entire conference week, but teachers who had seen our panel, or heard about it, came up to us in droves, excited to connect, to get informed, to take further action. TESOL formed a task force to address the issues our panel had raised and invited me to be on it.

Looking back on it now, I think it would have been wise to tell somebody – hotel security? – about the death threats, but at the same time I'm glad I didn't let fear deter me. I went on to give many workshops and talks for teachers in different states and countries, earn a PhD, become an academic, and write the first book on the subject: *Sexual Identities in English Language Education: Classroom Conversations.*[3] It's a research area that some still object to, which has made for a challenging, albeit rewarding, career. What has helped me speak out again and again is holding firm to a sense of purpose, a vision of the world that matters more to me than any discomfort I might feel as I work to bring that vision into being.

Speaking out does not necessarily mean being listened to, of course. Who gets to speak and who does not, who gets listened to and who does not – such matters are shaped by structural inequities involving race, class, caste, sexuality, gender, nationality, language background, dis/ability and so on. This is yet another reason why it can help to be driven by a vision of the kind of world one wants, as sustenance in the face of apathy and hostility.

*

March 2023. My living room in Sydney, papers spread across the rug. I was marking up the final edits of my first memoir, combing through the printed pages of my manuscript for what felt like the billionth time, making my final decisions, most of them minute: a comma here or a dash? This verb or that? Swap those two sentences or keep as is?

In a few months, *The Year My Family Unravelled* would hit the shelves of Australian bookshops.[4] I reached the last page and, exhausted but elated, splayed out on the sofa – the very place where, a few years before, my now-wife had read the first fifty pages of an early draft and, to my dismay, told me there was only one paragraph that sounded like me.

'I don't get any sense of the narrator,' she said. 'It's like you're not even there. Or like you're a neutral observer, reporting on things you saw and heard and did, but not what you thought and felt. You have to let readers *see* you.'

Her words had been a revelation: hard to hear but essential. They set me on a path of discovery, an arduous excavation. My memoir was about my family – the events of one particularly challenging year. My father, who lived overseas, had dementia and was in danger of falling, overdosing on his medication, getting lost, getting run over. As his only child, I wanted to help and protect him, but he fought my efforts, unable to comprehend (because of his dementia) that he had dementia and needed assistance.

During that tumultuous year, childhood memories threatened to overwhelm me.

It was an odd paradox: as my father was forgetting more and more of his life, I was remembering more and more of mine – not all of it good in relation to him, which made my role as his sole caregiver even more difficult.

But it wasn't until that day on the sofa when my partner gave me feedback on my early draft that I realised my memoir was not about my family, it was about *my* experience of my family. And I hadn't included what I felt or thought because I didn't know what that was. I had grown up observing my parents closely, studying their moods, identifying the triggers that made them anxious and upset, and intervening to try to keep the peace, but *I* didn't figure into it. In the same way that I'd disappeared myself in childhood, I'd been disappearing myself from my own memoir.

To tell my story in a way that would engage readers, I'd have to confront my lifelong habit of mentally and emotionally absenting myself when around my parents. It had protected me then; now it was a hindrance. I'd have to risk showing myself, risk seeing myself.

As I revised my manuscript, I set out to uncover the emotional truths that lay beneath my disappearing act. I went through the pages, tentatively at first, listening for the feelings, filling in the gaps, writing myself into scenes where I'd barely been present.

What helped to embolden me as I wrote (my keyboard wet with my tears) was telling myself (my younger self) that my life mattered too, that my experiences were worth articulating – for me, a potent message because as a child, I'd often felt worthless. What also helped was my unwavering commitment to telling my story as skilfully and honestly as I could – out of respect for the art form, for readers, and for the real-life people I was writing about.

By the time I finished the final edits and flopped across the sofa with sweet relief, I felt confident I had captured the story as it needed to be told. My memoir was published by Affirm Press in May 2023. Though I already had over thirty publications to my name, this memoir felt more me than anything I'd ever written, the voice unmistakably mine.

To my delight, readers have said my story has helped them face their own family dramas and traumas more courageously. Turning tough times into art has let me break through my own limitations and feel connected to people I've never met. Creative practice, I've learned, requires courage, but cultivates it too.

*

All those years ago when the school principal told my mother, in front of me, that I needed to come out of my shell, I said nothing, as usual, though inside I felt agitated, lost, alone. The difficulties of my childhood made me withdraw to protect myself. I led a lonely, self-berating existence. When I changed course in my mid-twenties and started to express myself, to assert myself, I was surprised to discover that I could do it. Perhaps my wilful muteness as a child – years of reading and attentive listening – fuelled my appreciation of the power of words.

Choosing a life of activism, education and writing has forced me to speak out in public – even when the process is emotionally gruelling, or my take on things is considered contentious. Channelling courage in different ways has allowed me to instigate changes that I want to see in the world and in myself.

I'd like to see more people feeling free to advocate for peace and justice. Raising uncomfortable topics. Telling complex truths. Refusing to be silenced, or to silence ourselves. Acknowledging the fear but taking action anyway. Drawing down that collective courage energy. Cracking open our shells. Creating a world where joy can flourish.

Doing What Needs to Be Done— Andrea Thompson

AB, CA, HMP, SXM, TRP

I have a strong sense memory of the first time I slept naked. I was around eleven and home from boarding school. The feeling of skin on cotton was simply delicious. Apart from when I was back at school, I never wore pyjamas again, until last year when my partner gave me a pair of PJ bottoms for my birthday. 'Nice and comfy for winter,' she said. I thanked her for the gift and, when she was gone, folded them up and put them away on a shelf in my walk-in wardrobe. I didn't realise it then, but I had no intention of ever wearing them.

One of the many things no-one ever discusses about the trans experience is the unexpected effects of gender-affirming hormone therapy. For us males to females, there is a welcome reduction in the size of the gonads and the appearance of breasts, softening of the skin, and redistribution of fat. All good, but what no doctor will ever tell you, probably because no trans woman will ever talk about it, is the effect of oestrogen on the simple act of urination. Though you're comfortably seated, the stream can still have a mind of its own, all that shortening of pipes ending up with urine going anywhere but into the porcelain. So, a few months later, deep into winter with my last pair of trackie daks soaked in recalcitrant pee, I went to put on the PJ bottoms. I was halfway through pulling up the second leg when I experienced a vivid flash of memory that transported me back to the then eleven-year-old me, wearing PJs and a dressing gown and being attended way too closely by one of my teachers. The memory was gone as quickly as it came, but it was as real as the night the abuse started.

Does surviving this experience make me a woman of courage? I hardly think so. Besides, we first must address the idea of whether I'm a woman at all. According to a good portion of the world, I am not. But I am. Defiantly so. I am female and I always have been. I've never needed any medical, psychological or legal intervention to be who I am. Gender is a social construct that has nothing to do with sex or anatomy. Notwithstanding, I've been through enough medical transition to be legally recognised as female here in Western Australia and I live full-time as me. Does that make me a woman of courage? No.

I existed for most of my almost sixty years in the cushioned palace of heterosexual male privilege. For many years I had a deep hatred of myself for not being able to reconcile who I was, so I paid a substantial price for my privilege, but I also was acutely aware of the advantage it brought me. Masquerading as a male, I was first in line for almost everything. I was unremarkably seen as superior to the other fifty-one percent of the population and no-one ever questioned the validity of my existence. I got ahead in the workplace, playing the classic breadwinner role to the detriment of my family responsibilities, and eventually reached a pinnacle in my career, becoming part of the executive leadership of one of Western Australia's largest public-sector organisations.

Eventually, my self-loathing caught up with me and I began to untangle my existence. My earliest memories begin at the age of four. One is of being held down by my grandfather in his chair in front of the TV while he rubbed himself against me. Another is of being female. At that age, I didn't have the language to process or understand either of these things. With the benefit of hindsight and a lot of talking to various counsellors, psychologists and psychiatrists, I now understand that the pervasive guilt, shame, and fear that I ascribed to my gender was born of the sexual abuse I survived in the family home and at boarding school. For decades, those emotions crushed every nascent attempt I made to express who I was, so I hid in the stifling luxury of my outward maleness and spent much of my life trying to annihilate my existence.

When I concluded that I didn't have the courage to erase myself, but I could no longer survive my self-loathing, I found a way to become, outwardly, the woman I have always been. After I came out people would ask me how it felt, and I would always answer the same way. I felt such joy and contentment. I was, for the first time in my life, happy and at peace. The weight was lifted from my shoulders.

These are the best years of my life.

However, from the moment of announcing my true self to the world, my life of privilege pivoted to something quite different. At first it was quite subtle and the bliss of being free carried me through those early moments when family and friends melted away. Then I began to deal with the labyrinthine intricacies of establishing my womanhood across all aspects of my life. That's when I realised that, in the eyes of most, I was not a woman at all, I was this other being whose existence they grudgingly permitted but could never understand. I was now a member of one of the most marginalised and oppressed groups in society.

I do not believe that my existence is an act of courage. I do not believe that people should love me just because I am gender diverse. What makes me (possibly) a woman of courage is what I do with my difference.

*

The precursor to my activism happened some years ago when, around four o'clock on a Wednesday afternoon, I was at Picabar in the heart of Perth's Cultural Centre to meet a musician who was looking for management and support with navigating an industry about which every cliché trotted out in that song by AC/DC is true. I've been a music journalist, promoter and manager for a good while now, and I'm always interested in working alongside talented artists. My conversation with that young, proudly queer woman and artist changed my life. As I listened to her speak about her journey, she said to me, 'The whole thing about you shouldn't walk alone at night, because you're a woman? No, I should do that, because you should feel safe. I'm willing to risk my life to stand for what is fair.' She meant it as well. It was the moment in our conversation that sealed our working relationship. It also made me think about what I needed to do with the rest of my own life.

As a gender-diverse woman, I hold a position of relative privilege. I am visible and I have no intention of ever taking a backward step. I also was gifted with an analytical mind: I've worked in jobs that gave me an understanding of politics and how things get done, and I'm a decent enough communicator. Having digested what this woman said to me, I decided I needed to live my life in absolute defiance of the current power structures and do everything I could to dismantle them. I don't want sympathy or special treatment, I simply want to live in a world where my gender is not used as a pretext for discriminating against me. I want governments to stop interfering in my life and to value my own expertise in being who I am. I demand the right to self-determination. I want this for all other trans and gender-diverse people as well. The time for us to hide is over.

My activism manifests in my life in the arts where I use the privilege of being a writer to foreground the trans experience and create stories and commentary that highlight the beauty and diversity of gender diversity, and that make our lives accessible to the mainstream. I want people to read my work and be challenged and confronted but to also see themselves in what they read because gender diversity is part of the human experience. I want to use literature to create a new normal.

I also use music and other art forms to create a platform for the visibility of LGBTQIA+ people and promote their excellence in the arts. My musician colleague and I now put on regular events that curate the best Perth has to offer in LGBTQIA+ musicians, DJs, comedians, poets, drag artists, artisans and creators. We deliberately put on these events in mainstream venues and advertise them as safe spaces for queer and gender-diverse people. By doing so, we're creating visibility and equity. Our ambition is to expand what we do so that we can support grassroots engagement in the arts and the careers of LGBTQIA+ artists and makers.

My need to more openly skirmish with the government increased in urgency when I started to work my way through the bureaucracies and organisations that have their tendrils wrapped around my existence, and I had to ask them for permission to simply be.

Change of name was the first port of call and, here in Western Australia, that requires a visit to the Registry of Births, Deaths and Marriages. Stepping out of the lift in the Registry's offices clutching a folder stuffed with the voluminous proof-of-existence documents required to make an application to change my name, I was greeted by a passing staff member who took one look at me and said, 'You're here to update your birth certificate: it's that way.' He moved on too quickly for me to address him and I was too stunned to speak anyway. I know he was trying to be helpful, but his immediate assessment of me was that I was trans, not a woman, and that he had the right to assume why I was visiting his workplace. For all he knew, I could have been there to announce my death, and I certainly died a little bit inside after he spoke to me. His was an act of prejudice, albeit unconscious and well intentioned.

This was my first in-the-wild encounter with cisgender privilege. To explain: those whose gender matches their genitals at birth are known as cisgender, cis for short. Being cis means never having to fight a raft of laws and organisational policies to establish your true identity. It means you will never be excluded socially and economically because of your gender, except, of course, if you're a cis woman. It means you will never face discrimination and violence because of your gender, except, again, if you are a cis woman. The term 'trans', as in 'transgender', translates from the Latin as 'across', 'beyond' or, my favourite, 'on the other side of'. Transgender people are deliberately classified as 'other' and that is one of many reasons why I reject the label, preferring, for the time being, 'gender-diverse'.

Cisgender privilege grants cis people a massive social and economic advantage over gender-diverse people. It comes from a place of omnipotence that by default excludes the worldviews of gender-diverse people because we are so far outside the realm of their experience that they have no reference for us. Usually, a cis person's only experience with gender-diverse people is the lurid and sensationalist media stereotypes that do nothing to illuminate our beautiful diversity. Even when a cis person is trying to be helpful, they are often also coercive, dismissive, bullying and ultimately harmful.

In Western Australia, the prime example of the harm that is caused by cis people is the legislation that was passed through Parliament in 2000 to establish the Gender Reassignment Board of Western Australia. The politicians, medicos, bureaucrats and other 'experts' who paved the way for the *Gender Reassignment Act 2000* (WA) intended the legislation to enable transgender people to have their gender legally recognised. As it stands, the law currently excludes many gender-diverse people as it only recognises two genders: male and female.

The full terror of the *Gender Reassignment Act* lies in its interpretation by the people appointed to the Gender Reassignment Board by the Attorney-General. A little more than ten years ago, two transgender men applied to the Board to have their gender recognised. Their applications were denied on the grounds that they needed to have hysterectomies before they could be legally recognised as male. They appealed the decision, which was eventually overturned by the High Court of Australia. If you're interested in learning more, a quick online search will give you the full story.

What is not addressed in the commentary about this case is that the Gender Reassignment Board chose to interpret and implement the *Gender Reassignment Act* as an enabler of state-enforced surgical mutilation. This was the ultimate example of the exercise of cis privilege when those who were entrusted with implementing this landmark legislation chose to use it as a means of imposing their cis worldviews and stereotypes of gender on the very people they were supposed to be helping.

On 16 April 2024, the WA government announced its intention to repeal the *Gender Reassignment Act*. At the media conference, the Attorney-General made a comment linking gender-diverse women to male sex criminals as justification for forcing applicants who are applying to have their genders legally recognised under the new system to undergo counselling. While repealing one oppressive law, the government signalled its intention to replace it with equally dubious legislation.

Are you outraged reading this? Most people I relate these facts to, including my gender-diverse colleagues and friends, respond – at most – with mild surprise. I suspect some of them think I'm overstating things. It seems that the cognitive dissonance these facts cause leads people to want to reject them. How could this possibly happen in a liberal democracy like Western Australia? Is this not more the staple of dictatorships like Nazi Germany? No, this is par for the course in most liberal democracies. It is real and it's happening right now.

I feel at my most isolated when people refuse to engage with the reality of the Gender Reassignment Board and its government-sponsored evil. A large part of me feels hopeless. I have written persistently to members of the state government over the last several years and, if I do receive replies, they simply trot out the party line, which is designed to mollify by saying that the government cares deeply about gender-diverse people and is doing all it can without going into specifics of what and when. These are lies.

When I finally understood that politely requesting that my rights be respected and enshrined in legislation would not be effective, I decided on a different course. In March 2024, I sent an email to all members of the current state government advising them that I had formally declared war on them and any organisation or individual who is working counter to the existences and rights of gender-diverse people. I told them that I would fight, until my last breath if need be, for complete decolonisation of the lives of gender-diverse people. By this, I mean that any laws that set out requirements for gender-diverse people that are different from what is required of cisgender people must be struck out.

I finished by saying that any member of parliament, organisation or individual who stands for anything less is a traitor to gender-diverse people and that a truce will only be possible when true equity is achieved.

*

At the time of writing, I am engaged in a campaign of direct action against the government that includes continued pressure through writing, public speaking and joining protests and online campaigns. I'm also taking radical action that I can't write about here. I consider myself to be a freedom fighter and will do whatever it takes to wake up the population to the government's continued and destructive exercise of power over the lives of gender-diverse people. This is now my life's work, and if I have to lay down my life early to achieve change, I will do so.

I still don't believe I'm a woman of courage. I'm just doing what needs to be done.

Endnotes and References

Introduction

1 Shakespeare, W. Act 1, scene 7, *Macbeth.*

The Sisterhood – Megan Krakouer

Sources and further reading:

ACOSS and UNSW Sydney. *Poverty in Australia 2022: A snapshot.* povertyandinequality.acoss.org.au/a-snapshot-of-poverty-in-australia-2022.

Amnesty International. 'The Overrepresentation Problem: First Nations kids are 26 times more likely to be incarcerated than their classmates'. 8 September 2022. amnesty.org.au/overrepresentation-explainer-first-nations-kids-are-26-times-more-likely-to-be-incarcerated.

Australian Institute of Family Studies. 'Effects of child abuse and neglect for children and adolescents'. Policy and Practice Paper, January 2014. aifs.gov.au/resources/policy-and-practice-papers/effects-child-abuse-and-neglect-children-and-adolescents.

Australian Institute of Health and Welfare. 'Income and Finance of First Nations People'. 7 September 2023. aihw.gov.au/reports/australias-welfare/indigenous-income-and-finance.

Australian Institute of Health and Welfare. 'Substance use among Aboriginal and Torres Strait Islander people'. 8 February 2011. aihw.gov.au/reports/indigenous-australians/substance-use-among-indigenous-people/summary.

Australian Government, Aboriginal and Torres Strait Islander Health Performance Framework, 'Tier 2: Determinants of Health. 2.08 Income'. indigenoushpf.gov.au/measures/2-08-income#.

Chamberlain et al. Supporting Aboriginal and Torres Strait Islander Families to Stay Together from the Start (SAFeST Start): Urgent call to action to address crisis in infant removals. *Aust J Soc Issues.* 2022 Jun; 57(2): 252–273. ncbi.nlm.nih.gov/pmc/articles/PMC9304314/ doi: 10.1002/ajs4.200.

Georgatos, Gerry and Megan Krakouer. 'The staggering suicide crisis billows unabated through our First Nations communities', *The Guardian*, 22 April 2024. theguardian.com/commentisfree/2024/apr/22/the-staggering-suicide-crisis-billows-unabated-through-our-first-nations-communities.

Gregoire, Paul. 'Indigenous youth suicide is a national crisis we're ignoring'. *The Big Smoke*, 12 May 2021. thebigsmoke.com.au/2021/05/12/the-suicide-of-indigenous-youth-is-a-national-crisis-were-ignoring-suicide.

Riley, Rob. 'From exclusion to negotiation: the role of psychology in Aboriginal social justice /discussion'. Paper (Curtin Indigenous Research Centre), No. 1/1997, Gunada Press, Curtin University, Perth WA.

Finding Strength – Averil Dean

1 Fisheries Department of Western Australia, *The Game Act 1912–1913*, s. 12A. 'Permit to Take and Kill Kangaroos for Food Purposes Only'.

How Women Shaped the World at the Beeliar Wetlands – Reneé Pettitt-Schipp

1 MacClaren, Lynn. 'Save Beeliar Wetlands Fact Sheet: 1 A Wetland Worth Saving'. Undated.

2 Drake, Cathy and Kennealy, Shona. 'Recollections of the Beeliar Wetlands'. Self-published booklet, sponsored by the City of Cockburn, Water and Rivers Commission (et al.), 1995.

3 MacLaren, op. cit.

4 'Roe8 Project Threatens Beeliar Wetlands'. Friends of the Earth Australia, 7 December 2016, foe.org.au/roe8_project_threatens_beeliar_wetlands.

5 Sartre, Jean-Paul. *Being and Nothingness: An Essay on*

Phenomenological Ontology. Richmond, Sarah (trans), 2nd ed. Routledge, 2003, p. 455.

6 Whish-Wilson, David. 'The Perth Freight Link: Stranger than Fiction'. *The Monthly*, 2 March 2017, themonthly.com.au/issue/2017/march/1488421058/david-whish-wilson/perth-freight-link-stranger-fiction#mtr.

7 Verstegen, Piers. 'Open Letter to Albert Jacob, Minister for the Environment', January 2017, in The Beeliar Group – Professors for Environmental Responsibility (February 2017). 'Urgent need for action: the Beeliar Group speaks out', thebeeliargroup.files.wordpress.com/2017/01/urgent-need-for-action-the-beeliar-group-speaks-out-170204.pdf.

8 Macy, Joanna and Johnstone, Chris. *Active Hope: How to Face the Mess We're in Without Going Crazy*. Finch Publishing, 2012.

9 Pipher, Mary. *The Green Boat: Reviving Ourselves in Our Capsized Culture*. Riverhead Books, 2013, p. 4.

10 'Deaths in Custody in Australia'. Australian Institute of Criminology, aic.gov.au/statistics/deaths-custody-australia.

11 Morrison, Della Rae. 'Dabakarn'. *Never Again: Reflections on Environmental Responsibility after Roe 8*. Edited by Gaynor, Andrea, Newman, Peter and Jennings, Philip. UWA Publishing, 2017, p. 75.

12 Garlett, Sealin and Abraham, Corina. 'The Significance of the Beeliar Wetlands for Aboriginal People'. *Never Again*, ibid., p. 45.

Learning to Swim – Eliora Avrahami

1 Carson, Rachel. *The Edge of the Sea*. Canongate, 2021, p. xi.

2 Irigaray, Luce. *Marine Lover of Friedrich Nietzsche*, Gilliam C. Gill (trans). Columbia University Press, 1991, p. 37.

3 Badiou, Alain with Nicolas Truong. *In Praise of Love*. The New Press, 2012.

4 ibid., p. 32.

Resistance as Courage – Sally Scott

1 Twain, Mark. *Pudd'nhead Wilson*. Prestwick House, 2006, p. 69.

2 Baird, Julia. *Phosphorescence: On Awe, Wonder and Things That Sustain You When the World Goes Dark*. Fourth Estate, 2020, p. 230.

3 ibid., p. 73.

Have Courage, Dear Heart – Shel Sweeney

1 This quote is inspired by the words whispered to Lucy by Aslan in C.S. Lewis' *The Voyage of The Dawn Treader*.
2 Lismore City Council. *Final Report. Lismore Flooding Impacts and Recovery Statement*. July 2022. lismore.nsw.gov.au/files/assets/public/v/1/2.-community/7.-emergencies-amp-disasters/documents/flood/lismore-flooding-impacts-and-recovery-statement.pdf.

I Don't Dance Like I Used To – Annamaria Weldon

1 Freadman, Professor Richard. Personal communication, 25 August 2023.
2 Weldon, Annamaria. 'At Lake Clifton, again – on being diagnosed with Parkinson's Disease'. *Cuttlefish*, Sunline Press, 2023, p. 11.
3 Freadman. op cit.
4 Brown, Brené. *I Thought It Was Just Me (but it isn't): Making the Journey from "What Will People Think?" to "I Am Enough"*. Avery, 2007.
5 'Dopamine', healthdirect.gov.au/dopamine.
6 Greene, Jordan and Caruso, Skyler. 'Michael J. Fox Says "Parkinson's Is a Gift" While Accepting Award for Best Documentary at National Board of Review Gala'. *People*, 12 January 2024, people.com/michael-j-fox-says-parkinsons-is-a-gift-best-documentary-national-board-of-review-8425920.

She Doesn't Seem Autistic – Esther Ottaway

1 Criado Perez, Caroline. *Invisible Women: Exposing Data Bias in a World Designed for Men*. Vintage, 2020.
2 Ottaway, Esther. 'The shamed body addresses its owner'. *She Doesn't Seem Autistic*. Puncher & Wattmann, 2023, p. 49.
3 Ottaway. 'Small talk'. ibid, p. 24.
4 Ottaway. 'Candles Unattended: a clinical history', ibid., p. 25.
5 Ottaway. 'Can't Keep House Woman', ibid, p. 44.
6 Ottaway. 'There's No Disabled Girls with Style Like Mine', ibid, p. 14. Reproduced online in *Rochford Street Review*, vol. 38, no. 1 (2023).
7 Garnett, Michelle to Esther Ottaway. Personal email, 4 August 2022.
8 Austin, Sarah to Esther Ottaway. Personal email, 29 Jul 2022.

9 Wood, Danielle. 'Poet Bravely Lifts the Lid on Life with Autism', *The Mercury*, 30 June 2023, pp. 40–41.

A Coin from the Man in the Moon – Natalie Damjanovich-Napoleon

1 'Endometriosis'. World Health Organization, 24 March 2023, who.int/news-room/fact-sheets/detail/endometriosis.
2 'Endo Myths (1980) vs Endo Facts (2018)'. Endometriosis Association.org, 2023. endometriosisassn.org/.
3 Jackson, Gabrielle. *Pain and Prejudice: A call to arms for women and their bodies*. Allen & Unwin, 2020.
4 Graham, Sarah. 'Pain & Prejudice: "Medicine needs to acknowledge that it has let women down"' [Q&A]. *Hysterical Women*, 8 January 2020, hystericalwomen.co.uk/2020/01/08/pain-prejudice-medicine-needs-to-acknowledge-that-it-has-let-women-down/.
5 Jackson, op. cit.

Breaking the Silence – Penny Jane Burke

1 World Health Organization. 'Devastatingly pervasive: 1 in 3 women globally experience violence'. Global, regional and national estimates for intimate partner violence against women and global and regional estimates for non-partner sexual violence against women. Developed by WHO and the UNDP-UNFPA-UNICEF-WHO-World Bank Special Programme of Research, Development and Research Training in Human Reproduction (HRP) for the United Nations Inter-Agency Working Group on Violence Against Women Estimation and Data. who.int/news/item/09-03-2021-devastatingly-pervasive-1-in-3-women-globally-experience-violence.
2 Australian Institute of Health and Welfare. 'Family, domestic and sexual violence in Australia, 2018'. Catalogue number FDV 2, AIHW, Australian Government, 2018, doi:10.25816/5ebcc144fa7e6.
3 Australian Bureau of Statistics. 4533.0 - Directory of family, domestic, and sexual violence statistics, 2018. abs.gov.au/ausstats/abs@.nsf/mf/4533.0.
4 Burke, Penny. 'Equitable Recovery: Generating Sustainable Higher Education for Equity and Social Justice'. Keynote delivered at the Global Higher Education Forum 2023, Malaysia. 14 November 2023.

From Penny Jane Burke: I would like to pay special and heartfelt tribute to the student victim/survivors who are participants in the UNESCO Chair in Equity, Social Justice and Higher Education project 'Understanding the Impact of Gender-based Violence on Access to and Participation in Higher Education' for the immense wisdom and knowledge they contribute. I would like to acknowledge the important contribution of the project team – Julia Coffey, Stephanie L. Hardacre, Jean Parker, Felicity Cocuzzoli, Julia Shaw and Adriana Haro – and our community partners, in our ongoing work to create a Gender Justice through Higher Education Hub. Thank you to Matt Lumb and Rhyall Gordon for their evaluative research in this space. I would also like to thank Kate Mellor, Regina Berretta, Matt Lumb and Matthew Bunn for their contribution to the Advancing Equity in the Sciences, Technology, Engineering and Mathematics in which gender inequalities and gender-based violence have emerged as key themes. Thank you to the wider team at the Centre of Excellence for Equity in Higher Education, who demonstrate enduring commitment to generating knowing and knowledge that challenges insidious inequalities and trauma in, through and beyond higher education. Finally, thank you to my family for their love and support.

Beyond 'Waste' and In/fertility – Nadia Rhook

1 For instance: 'The primary object of the VDL Company is to grow fine wool on the considerable portion of the waste and uninhabited lands of the island … if the company's ventures are a success, then it may be possible for them to grant aid to convert waste land into grazing land'. In 1825 *Van Diemen's Land Company. Return to an address of the Honourable House of Commons. Minutes of the arrangements between Early Bathurst, His Majesty's Secretary of State, and the Proposed Van Diemen's Land Company*. Great Britain. Parliament. House of Commons, 1825, Vol. XIX, p. 2. catalogue.nla.gov.au/catalog/7174706.

2 Bill for Vesting in His Majesty a certain Part of the Open Commons and Waste Lands, within the Manor or Royalty of Rialton and Retraighe, alias Reterth, in the Parish of Saint Columb major, in the County of Cornwall. 1817 Waste Lands Bill. The *Waste Lands Act*

(No. 5 of 21 Vic, 1857–8) was passed in Australia forty years later: see classic.austlii.edu.au/au/legis/sa/num_act/wla5o21v18578206.

3 Wollstonecraft, Mary. *A Vindication of the Rights of Woman With Strictures on Political and Moral Subjects*. London: J. Johnson, 1792. oll.libertyfund.org/titles/wollstonecraft-a-vindication-of-the-rights-of-woman.

4 Rhook, N. 'In the Jungle'. Unpublished. The final lines reference line 172 of T.S. Eliot's 'The Waste Land', which in turn plays on William Shakespeare's *Hamlet*, act 4, scene V, as spoken by Ophelia.

5 Haas, Lauren. 'The Revival of Myth: Allusions and Symbols in The Wasteland'. *Ephemeris*, vol. 3, article 8, Denison University, pp. 31–33, 2003, digitalcommons.denison.edu/cgi/viewcontent.cgi?article=1053&context=ephemeris.

6 'The Waste Land and the Fisher King'. Winding Way, wasteland.windingway.org/title/the-waste-land-and-the-fisher-king.

7 Rhook, Nadia. 'the day before egg collection'. *boots*. UWA Publishing, 2020.

8 Jackson, Michael. *Existential Anthropology: Events, Exigencies and Effects*. Berghahn Books, 2005, p. 93.

9 Clode, Danielle. 'Friday essay: who was Jeanne Barret, the first woman to circumnavigate the globe?'. 25 September 2020, theconversation.com/friday-essay-who-was-jeanne-barret-the-first-woman-to-circumnavigate-the-globe-146296.

10 There is extensive literature on queer ecological anti-colonialism. For instance, see Coomasaru, Edwin. 'Queer Ecologies and Anti-Colonial Abundance in Lionel Wendt's Ceylon'. *Art History*, vol. 46, no. 4, September 2023, pp. 750–776; Maxwell, Abby. 'On Witches, Shrooms, and Sourdough: A Critical Reimagining of the White Settler Relationships to Land' in *Journal of International Women's Studies*, vol. 21, no. 7, October 2020, pp. 8–22.

11 Rhook, N. 'In the Jungle'. op. cit.

On Breaking Out of Our Shells – Cynthia Dearborn

1 Participants of the Puget Sound Women's Peace Camp. *We Are Ordinary Women: A Chronicle of the Puget Sound Women's Peace Camp*. The Seal Press, 1985, p. 102
2 Carscadden, Lisa, Nelson, Cynthia and Ward, Jim. 'From silence to celebration: Lesbians and gays in ESL'. Colloquium, TESOL Convention, 13–17 April 1993, Atlanta, GA, United States.
3 Nelson, Cynthia D. *Sexual Identities in English Language Education: Classroom Conversations.* Routledge, 2009.
4 Dearborn, Cynthia. *The Year My Family Unravelled.* Affirm Press, 2023.

About the editor

Bron Bateman is an award-winning queer crip poet, editor and educator from Boorloo. She has had three collections of poetry published: *People From Bones* (with Kelly Pilgrim, Ragged Raven Press, 2002), *Of Memory and Furniture* and *Blue Wren* (Fremantle Press, 2020 and 2022). She has been published in journals such as *Westerly*, *Southerly*, *Cordite* and *Bent Stree*t and has performed her work locally, nationally and internationally. She has just completed her fourth collection. *Women of a Certain Courage* is her first edited anthology, and she is honoured and privileged to have had the opportunity to work alongside such brilliant women.

Contributors

Eliora Avrahami is an academic and poet interested in fictions of the self, living in Naarm with her wife and child.

Professor **Penny Jane Burke** is UNESCO Chair in Equity, Social Justice and Higher Education, Director of the Centre of Excellence for Equity in Higher Education and Global Innovation Chair of Equity at the University of Newcastle, Australia.

Lisa Collyer is a performance poet and educator in Boorloo (Perth). She writes poetry, with a lens on women's bodies. Her debut collection, *How to Order Eggs Sunny Side Up* (Life Before Man/Gazebo) was shortlisted for the Dorothy Hewett Award. She is published widely and has been a writer-in-residence for the City of Swan, The National Trust of WA, Katharine Susannah Prichard Writers' Centre and WA Poets Inc. She has recently appeared as a feature poet in Perth Writers Festival, Mandurah Readers' and Writers' Festival and York Writers Festival.

Natalie Damjanovich-Napoleon is a writer, singer-songwriter and educator who was raised on a farm by her Croatian immigrant parents. Her poetry and creative non-fiction have appeared in *Meanjin*, *Australian Book Review*, *The Australian (Review)* and *Australian Poetry Journal*. She has won the Bruce Dawe National Poetry Prize and the KSP Poetry Competition and has been shortlisted for the prestigious Peter Porter Poetry Prize and Penelope Niven Creative Nonfiction Award. Her debut poetry collection, *First Blood*, was released in 2019 and her second poetry book *If There Is a Butterfly That Drinks Tears* is out now via Life Before Man/Gazebo Books. Her work has been widely anthologised in the USA and Australia. Recently she completed a Creative Writing PhD on erasure poetry and cultural amnesia.

Averil Dean is a Menang Goreng Elder. Born in the bush at the Gnowangerup mission in 1939, she attended high school in Perth, and studied nursing at Royal Perth Hospital. While working at Broome Hospital, she met her husband-to-be, Kenneth Dean, and started a family. Feeling homesick, Averil moved, with the family, south to the Tambellup area to be close to her parents and extended family. Work commitments then saw Averil and Ken shift with their children to Cranbrook for twelve happy years. For educational benefits, they later relocated to Albany. In the early 1990s, brother Jack, Averil, and sister Treasy began teaching cultural studies at Albany Senior High School. Averil still works with schools as a cultural teacher. For fourteen years, Averil also worked for the Aboriginal Visitors' Scheme, supporting Noongar inmates at the Albany Prison. She draws strength from the resilience, hard work and love of her parents and family.

Cynthia Dearborn's debut memoir, *The Year My Family Unravelled*, was described in the *Saturday Paper* as 'fascinating … compelling'. She is also the author (as Cynthia D. Nelson) of *Sexual Identities in English Language Education: Classroom Conversations*. She has written for *The Guardian*, *Meanjin*, *The Weekend Australian*, and academic publications such as *TESOL Quarterly* and *The Oxford Handbook of Language and Sexuality*. She's been shortlisted for the Newcastle Poetry Prize and her play *Queer as a Second Language* has been performed in four countries. She's currently an honorary academic at the University of Sydney's Faculty of Arts and Social Sciences.

Jo Giles lives on unceded, Whadjuk Noongar boodjar in a converted railway carriage in Hamilton Hill. They share a house with Ross and Jacky Blue while they knit, collect sticks and write flash fiction and autobiographical poetry. Jo is a regular contributor to Perth Slam and in 2022, won the illustrious Perth Slam Cup. They have cystic fibrosis and, in 2015, received a bilateral lung transplant.

Anna Jacobson is an award-winning writer, artist, and researcher from Meanjin (Brisbane). She has written four illustrated books: a memoir – *How to Knit a Human* (NewSouth, 2024); and the poetry collections *Anxious in a Sweet Store* (Upswell, 2023), *Amnesia Findings* (University of Queensland Press, 2019), and *All Rage Blaze Light* is forthcoming with Upswell in 2025. In 2020 Anna won the Nillumbik Prize for Contemporary Writing and in 2018 she won the Thomas Shapcott Poetry Prize and the Queensland Premier's Young Publishers and Writers Award. She holds a Doctor of Philosophy in Creative Writing from Queensland University of Technology and received an Outstanding Doctoral Thesis Award. Anna's poetry chapbook *The Last Postman* (Vagabond Press, 2018) was part of the deciBels series 3. Her website is annajacobson.com.au

Megan Krakouer is a Menang person of the Noongar Nation who holds a Bachelor of Laws from Deakin University. She is Director of the National Suicide Prevention and Trauma Recovery Project, Director (Wagyl Kaip) of the South West Aboriginal Land and Sea Council, and works for knowmore, the free, independent legal service, contributing to the Royal Commission into Institutional Responses to Child Sexual Abuse. She is a renowned activist, prominent social justice advocate and arbitrator for the voiceless, and law reformer.

Paola Magni is an Associate Professor at Murdoch University, and a forensic scientist specialising in the application of natural sciences in crime scene investigation. Her research is primarily centered around forensic entomology, aquatic forensics, and best practices for managing challenging crime scenes, although her interests cross over into marine biology, anthropology, and trace evidence. Collaborating with scholars, law enforcement agencies, and institutions worldwide, she has made significant contributions to several high-profile cases.

Shannon Meyerkort is a West Australian author, bookseller and journalist, with a background is in the health and social sciences. She writes historical fiction for adults and chapter books for dyslexic readers. Her debut children's book, *Brilliant Minds: 30 Dyslexic Heroes Who Changed Our World* (Affirm Press), was published in 2022. She has been longlisted for the City of Fremantle Hungerford Award and was a finalist in the inaugural Best Australian Yarn short story competition. She was a 2022 KSP Writers' Centre Fellow and was part of the 2020 Fremantle Press/Four Centres Emerging Writers Program.

Esther Ottaway is a poet, editor and mentor who has won or been shortlisted for global prizes including the Tom Collins, Woorilla, MPU International, Mslexia, Bridport, Montreal, Tim Thorne Prize for Poetry and People's Choice in the Tasmanian Literary Awards. Her poetry is published in global journals, and she has coedited *Australian Poetry Journal*. Her acclaimed new collection is *She Doesn't Seem Autistic* (Puncher & Wattmann, 2023), and her previous books are *Intimate, Low-voiced, Delicate Things* and *Blood Universe*. In 2024 Esther will release a landmark anthology of disability writing, coedited with Andy Jackson and Kerri Shying, titled *Raging Grace: Australian writers speak out on disability* (Puncher & Wattmann, 2024).

Reneé Pettitt-Schipp is an award-winning writer who lived in the Indian Ocean Territories from 2011 until 2014. Her work with asylum seekers inspired her first collection of poetry, *The Sky Runs Right Through Us* (UWA Publishing, 2018), which was shortlisted for the inaugural Dorothy Hewett Award, and won the 2018 WA Premier's Prize for an Emerging Writer. Her non-fiction work about the islands, *The Archipelago of Us: A Search for Our Identity in Australia's Most Remote Territories*, was published by Fremantle Press in 2023. Reneé currently lives in Western Australia's Great Southern region.

Nadia Rhook is a white settler historian, poet, mother and educator, currently living in Naarm (Melbourne) on unceded Wurundjeri Country. Her writing appears in scholarly and creative places including *Postcolonial Studies*, Australian Poetry's *Best of Australian Poems 2022*, *Westerly*, *Portside Review* and *Cordite*. Passionate about imaginative ways of connecting with the past-present, Nadia is the author of two history-themed poetry collections: *boots* (UWA Publishing, 2020) and *Second Fleet Baby* (Fremantle Press, 2022).

Sally Scott was a perpetual student through the 1980s and 1990s, gaining a PhD in English Literature from the University of Western Australia. She has published *Fromage*, a cosy crime novel, and is working on a crime novel set in Tasmania. Sally lives in Perth with a husband, three spoiled felines and a huge number of books.

Shel (Michelle) Sweeney is a writer, counsellor/art therapist, editor and artist. She has worked for McGraw-Hill, Penguin Books and Heinemann, and in various educational and therapeutic settings. Shel lives on Bundjalung Country in the Northern Rivers region of NSW and works primarily in the mental health sector. Throughout her life, both art and writing have been pathways for Shel to make sense of the world, herself and her experience. Shel also delivers art- and writing-as-therapy groups, facilitates creative and therapeutic fibre-art workshops, leads writing groups for teens and is currently working on her own collection of poetry.

Andrea Thompson is a writer, music journalist and artist manager. She is the author of *Geraldine*, a novel that charts the ordinary life of an ordinary woman – or the extraordinary life of an extraordinary woman, depending on your perspective. She also is a contributor to *Spinning Around. The Kylie Playlist* (Fremantle Press, 2024). As well as a writer and arts worker, Andrea is a thorn-in-the-side activist, making herself equally unpopular with governments and LGBTQIA+ advocacy organisations by challenging their respective prejudice and timidity. The secret police dossier on her activities grows thicker by the day.

Annamaria Weldon was born in Malta and had lived in Africa, Britain and Central America by her tenth birthday. She began work as a newspaper feature-writer in 1978 and was first published as a poet (*Ropes of Sand*, Associated Press, Malta) in 1983. She has been published in journals and anthologies, among them *Purple Prose* (Fremantle Press, 2015), Weldon's awards include The Nature Conservancy Australia's inaugural Nature Writing Prize. She wrote *The Roof Milkers* (Sunline, 2008), *The Lake's Apprentice* and *Stone Mother Tongue* (UWA Publishing, 2014 and 2018) and is currently finishing a memoir.

MORE GREAT TITLES

Anne Aly, Liz Byrski, Sarah Drummond, Mehreen Faruqi, Goldie Goldbloom, Krissy Kneen, Jeanine Leane, Brigid Lowry and Pat Mamanyjun Torres are among fifteen voices recounting what it is like to be a woman on the other side of forty. These are stories of identity and survival, and a celebration of getting older and wiser, and becoming more certain of who you are and where you want to be.

'What I loved most about this book is how it joins the long tradition of women supporting, teaching, uplifting, and guiding other women. At the end of the day, young girls and women need role models – women who have lived long, full, and three-dimensional lives to learn from. And this book provides you with fifteen of them.' *Pelican Magazine*

MORE GREAT TITLES

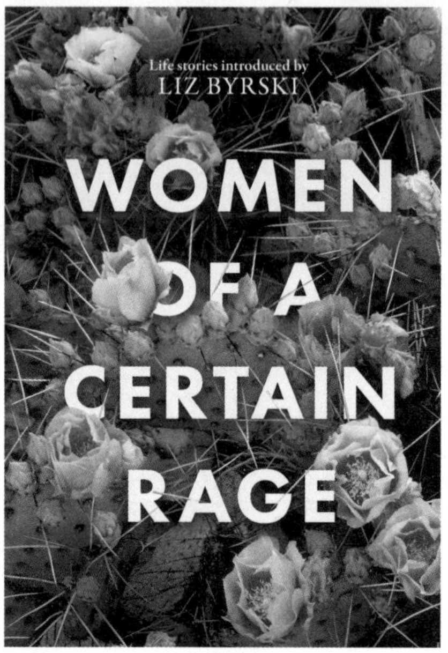

This book is the result of what happened when Liz Byrski asked twenty Australian women from widely different backgrounds, races, beliefs and identities to take up the challenge of writing about rage. The honesty, passion, courage and humour of their very personal stories is energising and inspiring. If you have ever felt the full force of anger and wondered at its power, then this book is for you.

'A great read. Rage has never been this compassionate, absorbing and thought-provoking.' *Judith Lucy*

'… its essays invite readers to engage with exciting thinking about rage's place in politics, relationships, and throughout a life.' *Australian Book Review*